The Entrepreneurial Way

92 Success Secrets and Shortcuts To Unleash
The Entrepreneur In You

Paul Breen

The Entrepreneurial Way

92 Success Secrets and Shortcuts To Unleash The Entrepreneur In You

ISBN 978-0-9943727-0-3

Printed in Australia

For further information please contact
www.paulbreen.com.au

To Dani, Samuel and Tommy who
inspire me every day…

Contents

Acknowledgements

A lot of people have helped me in my entrepreneurial journey. Too many to count have helped me start and/or build companies. And many more have encouraged me to speak, write about, help out and share what I know. A select few too have been on my back for three years to get this 'bloody book finally finished.' You know who you are…

It doesn't seem enough to just say thank you. But I genuinely do thank you. Your friendship and support has made my journey (so far) fun, memorable and worthwhile. And there's more to come…

Adam Cryer
Adam Knight
Amanda Levi
Andrew Crockett
Andrew Kerr
Angela Deva
Anna Winn
Anne Strange
Ash-lee Jones
Ashley Turner
Anthony Closter
Ay Giok Khoe
Barry Silverman
Ben Burge
Ben Rennie
Billy Adam
Bob Harvey (RIP)
Brett Gilbertson
Bruce Ryan

Cameron Ure
Chris Huntley
Chris Murphy
Chris Tait
Colin Oberon
Conor O'Malley
Courtney van der Weyden
Daniel Hillier
Daniel McSweeney
Danielle Holley
Dave Clerk
Dawn O'Neil
Dianna Butterworth
Dominic Leary
Earl d'Blonville
Emily Peal

Emma Johnson
Estelle Arts
Fiona Blayney
Gary Beck
Gary Cobbledick
Glenn Chandler
Glenn Rushbrook
Graham Anderson (RIP)
Graham Brown
Greg Nielsen
Gus Breen
Hendrik Vollers
Ian Draper
Ian Johnson
Jac Hunt
Jackie Wenck
Jacqui Warman
James Bolton

James Gerraty
James Grugeon
James Kyritsis
James Waldren
James Webber
Jamie Driver
Jan Ravnholt
Jen Miller
Jerome Gauder
Jim Meagher
Jimmy Livadiotis
Joanne Verry
John Edgar
John Lash
John Portelli
John Roach
Josh Phegan
Joyce Mathers
Julie Anne Breen
Kate Barrelle
Ken Edgar
Ken Fox
Kevin Toghai
Kevin Walker
Kitty Janssen
Leroy Soeterboek
Liam Walsh
Lizzie Howard
Marci McKenny
Margaret Breen
Marc Winkelman
Marina Paronetto
Mark Gronow

Mark Pittorino
(RIP)
Mark Vanzo
Matthew Baxter
Mic Lowne
Michael
Benveniste
Matthew Baxter
Michael Reif
Michael Ross
Mick Calder
Mike Ferrand
Mochtar Chia
Murray Gillin
Naomi Morton
Nic Georges
Paul Benveniste
Paul Hoffman
Paul O'Brien
Pete Bloomfield
Peter Arena
Peter Breen
Peter Littleboy
Phil Martin
Rachel Westaway
Rani Pattison
Rebecca Scott
Richard Brown
Richard Ellery
Richard Good
Rob Davies
Robyn Cowie
Ross Robinson

Ross Sheridan
Ryan Trainor
Scott Mitchell
Sarah Bartlett
Sarah Leslie
Sascha Schubiger
Scott Begg
Sean Rowlands
Selena Ward
Selwyn Becker
Simon Westaway
Stephen Small
Steve Jones
Steve Morgan
Stuart Grenville
Terry Cridland
Tim Stannage
Timothy Marc
Tom Cregan
Tony Conlan
(RIP)
Tony Sherburn
Tony Simmons
Vera Chan
Verne Davis (RIP)
Victoria Cain
Warren Nason
Will Fowles
William Morgan

Foreword

The wonderful reality in both teaching and researching entrepreneurship is that every so often one gets to meet the 'real' entrepreneurs—the amazing human beings who see opportunities most of us miss, and seem comfortable operating in environments of great uncertainty, risk and ambiguity while using the tools of perseverance, commitment and energy to craft their vision for the future.

Paul Breen is, in my view, one such outstanding entrepreneur.

Indeed, upon reading Paul's book *The Entrepreneurial Way*, I'm immediately struck by the thought, first described in 1985 by Peter Drucker, that "Entrepreneurship is neither a science nor an art. It is a practice".

Paul's entrepreneurial record is impressive. He's founded, launched or invested in several businesses over the past 20 years. Two became market leaders, and another has the potential to become one. For many people this might be enough, but Paul is working hard on incubating and developing three new opportunities as we speak.

Such is the life of the serial entrepreneur.

What Paul focuses on is uncovering waste and inefficiency in a market. Where customers are being overcharged or underserved. Where there's potentially a large pool of untapped demand. Where, with a different approach or service delivery model, an opportunity can be unlocked.

The Entrepreneurial Way describes this process, not as a given 'on-a-plate' opportunity but rather as a disciplined approach of trial and error, hard work and in-market testing to shape it into a high-potential venture with a product customers will willingly pay for. At its core is the need to think and do things differently to conventional business managers.

Paul's book brings these lessons to life. Serial entrepreneurs such as Paul typically devise ingenious strategies to marshal their limited resources to provide a sustainable and meaningful service the community not only uses, but *values*.

This wonderful book provides an experiential exploration of how entrepreneurs think and act. How they approach risks and opportunities. How they build and manage teams. How they turn an idea into a market-leading business. It also describes the mindset required to be successful.

The book is divided into 92 individual lessons so powerful that each one needs to be read and pondered before moving on to the next. The lessons are all insightful and meaningful no matter what your circumstances are, the stage of your career or whether you work for yourself or for someone else.

Enjoy this life-changing read, and commit yourself to acting entrepreneurially in your approach to life, work and other pursuits.

And finally, Paul's book will now become recommended reading for all of my future students.

Emeritus Professor L Murray Gillin AM

Entrepreneurship and Innovation, Swinburne University of Technology

Melbourne, 15th June 2015

My Story

In 1995 I invested $30,000 to start my own business, a seasonal retail chain called Calendar Club. It was all the money I had, and if Calendar Club didn't work out I'd be broke. I had no retail experience, and in the early days I had to work full-time to support myself.

I started the business from the second bedroom of my rented apartment, without staff or even a computer. And soon after I cut the safety net and left my job.

Eight years later I sold to Australia and New Zealand's largest book chains. Along the way the business pioneered 'pop up retail' in both countries, and achieved a 35% market share. Today, the business continues to prosper, operating 150 stores every year. It's never been successfully copied or replicated, and no other seasonal retailer has reached its scale or size.

This book is all about my 20 year roller-coaster ride as an entrepreneur and what I've learned along the way.

The Journey

In 1994 I was sitting in my cubicle at Mobil Oil, wondering whether I'd be the next one to get a tap on the shoulder and a redundancy cheque. The company had already been through two restructuring rounds in the previous three years, and the carnage still hadn't stopped. I knew my number would come up sooner or later, and so I needed to start making plans.

After 10 years in corporate life, I needed something different. I was tired of the politics, the arse-covering and the focus on short-term results. I had a good job and worked with some great people, but too many other factors were dragging me down.

I didn't know what else to do. But I *did* know I had to get moving.

I rang a few recruitment companies, and even went for a couple of job interviews. But nothing really inspired me.

Around the same time I began visualising what I wanted my future to look like. And it was easy enough to do. I wanted to work somewhere that had an inspiring, can-do culture where I had more control over what I did. A place without all the stuff I hated about corporate life. A place where the team chased lofty goals, and where excellence and results were rewarded.

The search for the next stage of my career suddenly became a lot simpler. There were really only two options:

- get a job in a small, growing business in tune with my needs
- start a business myself, and create the type of business I've always wanted to work at.

After a few weeks of soul searching, I decided to back myself and start my own business. I didn't know where to start, but the decision felt right to me.

And so began my long search for a suitable business opportunity.

Google was years away from being launched so you had to research the old-fashioned way by wearing out shoe leather.

I pored over everything from business opportunity magazines to industry research papers. I met tons of people, drank gallons of coffee, and learned a lot.

After 12 months of hard work I had a shortlist of business opportunities that I could start without a lot of money. And that was important, because I didn't *have* a lot of money.

Calendar Club, a fledgling US concept retailer looking to expand through international licencing, came closest to fitting my requirements. It was a tall order, but I went ahead anyway and started my first business.

It was 1995. I was 31 years old, hadn't worked in retail, and only had a small network of business contacts.

Most of my family and friends thought I was crazy to leave a great job to sell calendars, and in some ways I could see their point. But I'd done my homework, and went ahead with it anyway. In fact, their negative comments actually spurred me on.

I learned a lot of important lessons in that first year.

The first lesson was about geography. My initial container of inventory and shop fittings was shipped from the port of Galveston in Texas, and was due to arrive in Melbourne 24 days later. But the container somehow made its way to Johannesburg in South Africa.

After months of careful planning, this was unbelievable. I was furious. With my three trial stores due to open in less than three weeks I had to do some fast talking with the shopping centre managers and our prospective store managers.

We also had to work out how to quickly get the container from Johannesburg to Melbourne.

My customs broker madly worked the phones, and managed to get the container transferred to a ship bound for Melbourne. Unfortunately its first port of call, Perth's Fremantle port, was shut down at the time due to a wharf strike.

After sitting off Fremantle for several days, the shipping company decided to skip it altogether and head to Adelaide. Rather than wait any longer, I arranged for the container to be unloaded at the Adelaide docks and transported to Melbourne by truck.

After arriving late on the Friday night, we spent the entire weekend getting everything organised. It was a massive effort, but all three stores opened on the Monday. It was a huge achievement, and I convinced myself the worst of it was finally over.

It wasn't.

Within half an hour of the stores opening I'd received calls from two of the shopping centre managers, telling me they'd terminated my lease and I needed to close down by the end of the day because competing retailers were threatening lawsuits if we were allowed to continue trading.

After nine months of preparation, I could see the business crumbling before my eyes.

Facing financial ruin while still trying to manage my full-time job, I negotiated for the stores to keep trading until the end of their lease periods. It took a careful blend of diplomacy and sheer bloody-mindedness. I needed to compromise enough to pacify the centre managers without crippling the business.

For example, one kiosk had to be moved seven times to appease local retailers. Each move took three hours with four people, and had to be done outside of normal trading hours. At one point we did four moves in six days.

Another kiosk had to be relocated to another shopping centre 41 kilometres away.

At this point I was exhausted, my nerves were frayed, and I was ready to pull the pin. But then one of our store managers called me to say the mall's security guards had been instructed by the centre manager to move our kiosk again (for the eighth time) after the centre closed. What's more, they were moving it to the worst possible location in the centre without even asking for permission.

After ringing the centre manager to confirm the story, I arrived at the shopping centre with a strongly worded legal letter saying it would be in their best interests not to touch the kiosk. My lawyer came too, saying he "wasn't going to miss out on any of the fun".

Having narrowly averted the problem, my resolve strengthened. There was no way I was stopping now and I managed to trade all three stores until the end of their lease periods without further disruption.

At the end of the selling season I had to make a decision: stay in my well-paid job and pursue a corporate career, or resign and try and build my business. The three stores racked up $200,000 in sales over seven weeks and the business had broken even —it was just enough to suggest it was a reasonable business opportunity.

But the difficulties we'd faced (particularly with the shopping centres) tempered my view somewhat.

After careful consideration, I decided that if I could increase the business to ten stores and $1m in annual sales it was worth doing. This became my first goal, and I left my job to get on with it.

With no team, no structure and limited funds this goal seemed almost unattainable. But having just cut off my job lifeline, I had no choice other than to succeed.

No-one had tried building a large-scale seasonal retail business in Australia before, so I was moving into unchartered waters. (The term 'pop-up' wouldn't exist for another ten years.) Fortunately, shopping centre owners didn't understand the true value of their prime common-area retail space back then, and were giving it to sitting tenants for nominal rent, if not for free. This worked in my favour, as it gave me time to develop the business without being crippled by excessive occupancy costs.

Mind you, with only a handful of local calendar publishers back then the range of calendars available was very limited. A couple of publishers dominated the supply chain, and newsagents were the main re-sellers. I wanted to create a retail category killer for calendars, which meant I needed at least 1,000 suitable titles. But in 1995 there were only about 300 titles worth buying. So not only did we have to set up the retail side of the business, we also had to help build 'content' with our suppliers and publishers.

(Today the business has more than 3,500 titles for sale.)

The combination of 'cheap' retail space and the latent (under-served) consumer demand for calendars which we hoped existed, gave us a tremendous opportunity.

But we needed to move quickly. Securing shopping centre sites was the name of the game, and we went for it—hard.

In the second year we opened 21 stores in Australia and eight stores in New Zealand. By then, I'd added one full time staff member and a part-timer and outsourced virtually everything else. The business was held together by sticky-tape and chicken wire. Our businesses processes were almost non-existent, and we lurched from one crisis to the next. The working hours were crazy and I didn't have a day off for ten months. It was one of the hardest years of my life, and if something could go wrong, it did.

Amazingly, at the end of the selling season we had sales in excess of $2m and had made a small profit. We were on our way, and having blasted through the ten-store goal we decided to aim higher.

I remember reading *Built to Last: Successful Habits of Visionary Companies* by Jim Collins and Jerry Porras. The book talks about establishing 'big hairy audacious goals' or BHAGs—massive goals that stretch your capability and capacity. They're not easy to achieve, but they're not meant to be.

We needed a BHAG, and decided that having 100 stores was a pretty good one.

Then reality set in. We had no idea how to build, finance and operate a 100-store retail chain. 29 stores had stretched the company's capabilities to the limit.

If we were serious about it, we needed to understand the growth path to 100 stores and what needed to happen at every stage along the way.

Standing in my office, I put a sign on one wall that said '29 stores'. On the other wall I wrote '100 stores'. Standing at that '100 stores' sign and looking back at the '29 stores' sign, I suddenly realised the enormity of our task. We were 71 stores short.

Thinking about the challenge, it became clear we needed to think of anything that could stop us achieving the 100-store goal. What impediments could we face along the way, and how would we overcome them? Basically, we needed to begin at the end and work backwards.

We came up with a lot of potential challenges. But this approach made the future far more predictable.

We started by working out the structure we needed to operate a 100-store business, looking at every aspect of the business and leaving no stone unturned. That gave us a list of actionable tasks to complete, and we drew up a timeline for achieving them. From there we gave everyone responsibilities, and reviewed our progress regularly.

Essentially, we transformed the BHAG into a set of strategic initiatives, and then into a detailed step-by-step operational plan. Based on what needed to be done and the business' current condition, we estimated that we'd need another six years to build a structure robust enough to successfully operate 100 stores. (We did it in four.)

Along the way we had to bring in a new strategic partner, raise extra funds to finance our expansion and overcome many operational challenges. Balancing the needs of short-term survival against moving towards the BHAG created tension at times. But that tension helped us focus on the end game and avoid getting distracted.

If we hadn't been smart, resilient and uncompromising, we would have failed. On numerous occasions we had to 'stare down' the owners of big shopping centres who were making unreasonable demands. Any sign of weakness and we would have faced skyrocketing rents, been shunted into secondary mall locations, and become a punching bag whenever another retailer complained about us.

But we didn't buckle, and always found a way to leave a bad discussion on good terms.

One year (~2000) a major shopping centre group tried to put our rents up by 60%. Not only that, they tried doing it at the last minute after we'd already committed to large stock purchases and other commercial contracts. Agreeing to these demands would have been disastrous. It would have seriously compromised our current trading season, and once word got around the other shopping centre owners would have followed suit the next year. It would have been economic slaughter for us.

I called the guy responsible, and he reluctantly came to my Melbourne office to talk about it. He was nervous—his leg began to shake during the meeting. While I was like ice on the surface I was very nervous too. I knew how important this meeting was for our future.

I calmly explained what we were prepared to do regarding the rent rises—a 12% increase, spread over two years. He said he was under pressure to deliver 60%. We batted it around for a while, but didn't make any real progress.

Reaching under my desk, I grabbed the keys to our warehouse and threw them in his lap. I told him he may as well take over because I'd never agree to terms like that, and that we'd wind back our local business and sell our product overseas.

Importantly, he believed me and two days later we agreed to a 15% rent increase, spread over two years.

I knew he couldn't afford to lose the Calendar Club account at such late notice. We were the biggest seasonal retailer, and were growing rapidly. At the time there weren't any other national seasonal programs operating, so they couldn't replace us easily. I forced him to become an ally, and he had to take up the fight within his company on our behalf. He did, and we lived to fight another day.

We had no real power. But we had brains and balls, and that was enough to ensure our prosperity.

When I first left the business in 2003, the business was operating 140 stores and was worth hundreds of times its 1995 value. Even now, in 2015, it's still Australia's largest, most enduring and most successful seasonal retailer.

Looking back it's hard to believe that a business trading out of small kiosks (no larger than 16 m2) for only 10 weeks a year, and selling a $20 item could rack up sales in excess of $350m since it started. And still be growing.

That makes me smile (and feel a little bit proud).

After the Sale

By the age of 40 I'd started and exited a market-leading business. With a great team we'd built a company that changed the retail environment by introducing pop-up retail (at scale) as a viable business model. Other pop up businesses have emerged since then, but we were the first and are still the biggest and most successful.

After Calendar Club I took six months off to spend time with my family, and it was a wonderful time in my life. But it wasn't long before I was thinking about what to do next.

And I didn't have a clue.

I'd been so busy building Calendar Club I hadn't even considered what I'd be doing in the new millennium. But what quickly struck home is that I didn't have a professional network of friends and advisors who could help me in the future. The phone had stopped ringing.

Fortunately, a great friend Tom Cregan had, a year or so before, started his own business called EPAY Australia, an electronic payments business focused on pre-paid transactions for mobile phone top-ups. Tom is one of the smartest people I know—an MBA graduate with senior corporate experience with Mobil Oil, Optus and Westpac.

While helping Tom with a difficult transaction early on, I decided to invest in the business. It was a fortuitous decision as EPAY became the largest business of its type in Australia, reaching annual sales of $400m before it was sold to a listed USA company. Investors received more than ten times the return on their original investment, and the company grew to a 90% market share with annual revenue of $2bn.

Following the success of Calendar Club and EPAY, I co-founded a small boutique investment business. Its purpose was to acquire small-medium sized businesses from owners looking to retire.

On paper it looked like a winner. Research suggested a growing number of ageing business owners were looking to cash out and retire. The economy was booming, and money was everywhere. Bank debt was plentiful and available, and cashed-up investors were looking for deals to deploy their capital.

The problem was that good deals (or rather deals that represented anything like good value) were few and far between. Vendors were delusional about the value of their businesses. They were happy to sell, but you had to over-pay if you wanted to buy.

We didn't.

We spent eighteen months trying to buy a business. From almost 200 potential opportunities we looked at 20 closely, made offers on six, and managed to buy one.

And that deal (a co-investment with a private equity firm to acquire a niche supermarket chain) turned out to be a disaster.

It was an interesting experience for me. Up to this point, everything I'd been involved with had been a success.

The business seemed viable, the team we assembled looked solid, and the strategy was sensible. Unfortunately the execution was terrible. The board lacked unity, and the management team couldn't translate the strategy into a deliverable operational plan. Tough decisions that needed to be taken were deferred, and money was wasted on non-productive activities.

In early 2009 it suddenly dawned on us all that the business could actually fail. But even that didn't stop us procrastinating because we couldn't agree what to do.

A board restructure finally meant we could make some decisions, and I volunteered to roll up my sleeves. We needed to take drastic action immediately to save the business, and we didn't believe the management team could do it on their own. I worked with the remaining board members on a restructure plan to save the business.

And then I was given a mandate to carry it out.

Suddenly (and unintentionally) I was in charge of the business as the interim CEO, and ultimately responsible for quickly turning it around. Within days I discovered massive inefficiencies and bad practices. Some of the senior management team (including the incumbent CEO) had to be let go, and several other staff members either left or were made redundant. The remaining team then spent four months fighting to save the business.

Unfortunately we ran out of both cash and time, and were forced to call in the administrators. Another six months with the support of our suppliers and we would have made it. It truly was a heartbreaking moment for everyone involved.

I've often thought about whether I should have taken the easy option—resign as a director and leave the problem to someone else to solve. But I couldn't resist trying to fix it and I thought we had a fighting chance. With hundreds of jobs on the line and a range of problems to fix, it was always going to be tough. And I knew failure, ridicule and enhanced personal liability were all possibilities.

But those personal risks were less important to me than trying to save the business. And while it didn't work out, I know I'd do it again.

The Pull Strategy

Having experienced my first failed business venture, I made a decision. If I was going to invest or otherwise become involved in any new business or opportunity I'd do it patiently, and from the inside as an invited party.

My investment company experience turned me off using business brokers and corporate advisors to bring deals to me. I didn't like the process—it was difficult and time consuming, and depending on the advisor the information memorandum would either be a carefully prepared document that actually reflected reality, or a rush job that was fanciful (if not downright inaccurate).

Mostly, at least back then, you were presented with heavily shopped-around deals that were either overpriced or poor quality. I'd been down that path before, and I wasn't anxious to repeat it.

Instead I had to seek out and create new opportunities myself. But how could I get invited 'inside the tent'?

First of all I needed to raise my profile. I'm not a natural self-promoter, so I needed a way to become better known without comprising my authenticity. I decided on a 'pull strategy', where people would seek me out instead of me having to overtly promote myself. And the only way to do that was to provide something valuable to a wide audience that's normally hard to find.

And then one day it came to me—I'd start blogging about my business experiences. Starting with a small email list and writing under the pseudonym of 'The Bull' I wrote short, pithy, truthful articles each week about the realities of business, based on my own experiences.

Progress was slow to start with, and my distribution list didn't grow for a long time. But after sticking with it for more than three years momentum started to build. More than three hundred articles later, many of my blog posts have been read and shared by tens of thousands of people worldwide.

People have told me the articles helped them in their careers and their businesses. Others have said my writing gave them a deep insight into my character. They felt like they knew me, and what I stood for, even though we'd never met. And I still get pulled aside at functions to discuss something I wrote in a past article.

What helped was writing an article virtually every week for five years that landed in my readers' inboxes every Monday morning. It was tough to do at times, but the discipline and regularity created familiarity with readers and, eventually, a cyber-relationship of trust and comfort. (Or so I've been told.)

By openly sharing my successes and failures I gradually achieved what I set out to create—a pull strategy where opportunities came directly to me. And while it took longer than expected, it worked better than I thought possible.

Recent Adventures

This pull strategy led to a myriad of opportunities that would never have come my way if I hadn't become a blogger. Many times I'd get an email from someone on my distribution list wanting to discuss a business problem or opportunity they were facing, or a referral to someone in the same situation. This inevitably led to me providing some free advice, and on many occasions to coaching and advisory work. In fact, between 2009 and 2014 I coached or advised more than 20 companies of various sizes—some of them for long periods of time.

In 2012 I was tapped on the shoulder to become the start-up CEO of Powershop Australia, a new disruptive electricity retailer owned by the ASX-listed company, Meridian Energy Ltd. It was my first ever 'intrapreneur' role, and I was given the mandate to lead the launch of the business into the Australian market.

When I started at Powershop the business had 39 retail customers, a team of six and no brand awareness. I went into this role with my eyes wide open knowing that, like any start-up, the first 1,000 or 10,000 customers is always the toughest to get. This was made even more difficult by operating in the most competitive retail electricity market in the world.

However, despite the tough market conditions and the *normal* pressures of a start-up we created strong momentum in a crowded market and grew to 15,000 customers within 12 months of our public launch (exponentially increasing to 55,000 a year later).

We also built high brand awareness and carefully put in place a strong, motivated team to carry the business forward.

Powershop's success was a direct result of a fantastic team effort and a commitment to *build it right* from day one. We eschewed the *questionable* industry conventions of door-knocking and cold calling people at home. Instead we established a genuine sales (not *salesy*) culture based on four key premises:

- Work with 'warm leads' only. This meant we had to establish strong partnerships in the market with organisations that could bring business to us.
- All team members either had to serve the customer or serve someone who does. No exceptions.
- All customer 'wins' had to be without 'shame'. That is, we must be proud of our actions.
- Any customer losses had to be without regret. If customers choose to leave us it won't be because we let them down.

We also invested in irreverent, eye catching and thought provoking advertising campaigns to wake up the market and get noticed. Critical too was the fact that our prices were highly competitive. And, of course, at every level we were unapologetic about holding people (anyone) accountable to deliver what they promised.

It was a tough, uncompromising approach. Standard practice for a start-up. And it worked a treat. The company's continuing success is testament to that.

I also chaired the advisory board of Real Institute, a leading Australian training company that was sold to a listed Australian company in 2014 for $54m. This was a phenomenal outcome considering the business was started seven years earlier with capital of $50,000.

I was also invited to stay involved with the international development of the Calendar Club franchise, which operates across six countries and 1,500 stores, by chairing the Group International Advisory Board for four years.

And for more than four years I've been a board member of the award-winning social enterprise Streat, providing life-changing opportunities for disadvantaged and homeless youth in Victoria.

Along the way I co-founded Australia's first innovation lab and collected active investments in a fast-growing online insurance brokerage, an award-winning blog and a peer-based online review service for the workplace.

My latest project—the Breen Institute—is a labour of love. I founded this education business to teach organisations and individuals how to innovate better and faster using design thinking, a problem-solving and opportunity creation method I've used my entire career.

And I'm really excited about it.

Back to the Future

In February 2011, following a record sales year with strong profits, Calendar Club went into voluntary administration. The business hadn't done anything wrong, and should have never been in this situation. The problem was it was owned by Red Group Retail, who also owned Angus & Robertson, Borders and Whitcoulls (NZ). And when they went broke, Calendar Club got caught up in the mess.

The outcome was a debacle, and a horrible waste of investors' money. Angus & Robertson and Borders were both liquidated, and Whitcoulls was sold. Fortunately I was given the opportunity to re-acquire the business, and I led the team to do just that, finally completing the deal in August 2011.

Almost eight years after leaving the business, and 16 ½ years after founding it, I was now back in charge. Talk about serendipity.

The Price You Pay

Looking back on my 20 years as an entrepreneur, I could hardly call it a glamorous life. The idea of working hours to suit and taking time off whenever I wanted was a pipe dream, at least for the first decade. Instead it was a game of inches, with many frustrations and disappointments along the way. Momentum seemed to take forever to build, and I often wondered whether I should give up and get a job.

The first few years involved working late nights and weekends endlessly. I lived in constant fear of meeting the weekly payroll bill, and often woke in a cold sweat worrying that a 'monster' competitor would suddenly emerge and destroy my business.

I felt guilty for a long time because I was a crap boyfriend, never able to do anything socially with my girlfriend (now wife) or our friends because I was working all the time. I gave up all of my hobbies and other interests because I didn't have time to focus on them. I had no money, drove an old bomb, ate $5 Thai takeaway most nights, and my credit cards were always maxed out.

Many entrepreneurs I know have a similar story. It seems to be a common price to pay to achieve something worthwhile.

So was it worth it? Absolutely. And I'd do it all over again if I had to. Sure it's a big sacrifice, especially early on, but if it works it can change your life.

And that's reason enough to give it a red-hot go.

What's Next?

So what's next?

I have no idea. I've never planned more than 12 months ahead, and it's worked fine for me so far.

However, since turning 50 not so long ago I've decided to tweak a few things. I'll increase the pace of what I choose to do and do fewer things that feel repetitious. I'll set hard short-term goals, and push myself to achieve them. I'll keep learning, and forcing myself to do things that are new and difficult. And I'll only choose opportunities and causes I find interesting, stimulating and worthwhile.

I'll spend less time in airplanes and more time with my family. I'll see my parents and my mates more regularly, and let them know how important they are to me.

I *won't* be changing my 12-year-old Mitsubishi or my $12 haircuts, and you definitely won't see me wearing suits too often. And I doubt I'll start worrying about what people say about me.

I want to keep pushing out my comfort zones and taking risks. I don't know whether I'll succeed, but I certainly won't die wondering.

And hopefully, when my time's finally up, I can honestly say I've lived a life with few regrets. Time will tell.

Why I Wrote This Book

I wrote this book to share the things I've learnt in three decades in business. Things I wish I'd known back when *I* was starting out.

It doesn't matter whether you work for yourself or for someone else. Or the size of the business you are involved with. The lessons are all relevant no matter what your circumstances.

What I genuinely believe is that the ability to think creatively and apply an entrepreneurial mindset to any problem or opportunity is the key to your future success.

These 92 success secrets and shortcuts are a collection of lessons, anecdotes, insights and observations that address the issues about business and life that really count. It's a blend of home-spun philosophy and practical DIY no-nonsense suggestions.

You can read them individually or in combination, and in any order. Hopefully you'll refer to them regularly.

Some will be uplifting, while others may cause mild discomfort. But if you want a book that's grounded in reality and can really help you achieve business success, this is it.

Now, grab a highlighter and read on.

The Secrets and Shortcuts

About 'You'

Before you start researching business opportunities, there's something else you need to find out about.

Or rather, someone.

You.

In many respects, you don't just own the business. You are the business. So you need to know exactly who you are, what you stand for, what you value, and what you won't put up with. And then you need to stay true to yourself, no matter what happens.

You also need to remember why you became an entrepreneur in the first place. Yes, you'll have to work hard for seemingly little reward at first. And you may have to deal with your fair share of naysayers. But stick with it, because it will be worth it in the end.

Make sure too you own the business, instead of it owning you. And remember success isn't just measured by how much you make but rather what you are made of.

Just Be Yourself

I like to wear t-shirts and jeans whenever I can. It's rare for me to don a suit, even when conducting official business. And ties are useless, pointless rags.

I've been this way for more than 20 years. It frustrates my wife sometimes, especially when we're supposed to be 'dressing up' for a night out. But I can't help it—it's what I'm comfortable in.

It can create an interesting dynamic when you meet people for the first time. Some pay attention to your casualness, discreetly looking you up and down while trying not to act surprised. And some automatically underestimate you and your capabilities—shallow, but understandable.

I don't think there's anything wrong with dressing up or down. It's a personal choice. Steve Jobs did it consistently with his trademark blue jeans, black turtleneck top and New Balance runners. It was his outfit of choice and it never changed. It was comforting and timeless, and became as recognisable as the products Apple developed.

Maybe it was his way of saying, "I'll dress how I want, and this is comfortable to me" or "I make decisions every day, so I'm paring them down to the ones I care about. And what I wear isn't one of them."

Or maybe it was deeper than that. "I'm just like you. I talk like you. I dress like you. I understand you. I'm not going to change, and neither is Apple."

Whatever it was, it worked. It created consistency, which is important. It conditioned people to know what to expect of him, and that there wouldn't be any surprises.

And the same is true of the company he co-founded. Apple produces great products that delight customers. And it does it consistently. It's as simple as that.

Wear whatever suits you best and that you're comfortable in. Always remember, however, that the true measure of a person lies in what they do, not what they wear.

The same applies to using flowery language or corporate-speak instead of plain English. If you decide to speak like an English Professor, then you'd better have the stuff to back it up.

Being yourself means being authentic—a highly prized asset. You have to accept that you're not perfect, and have vulnerabilities and weaknesses just like everybody else. But this doesn't mean you shouldn't emphasise your uniqueness and special qualities. It means you should be just as open about your failures and weaknesses as you are about your successes and strengths. Doing this gives your personal story the humanity that lies at the heart of behaving authentically.

Many of these lessons only become clear as you get older and after you've collected a few 'scars' on the way through.

What I do know is that substance wins over fluff every time, at least in the long term.

But what's the difference between the two?

To me, it means never doing things in private that you'd be embarrassed to be made public. And being honest even when no-one else is watching.

It means you don't care two hoots about the superficialities of wealth, status, power, fame, or the promise of 'the next big thing'. You don't talk about money (yours *and* other people's), and you don't care about 'keeping up with the Jones".

And you feel perfectly comfortable turning up to a red carpet event in a clapped-out 1985 Ford Laser.

It means always trying to do the right thing.

You treat everyone the same too, whether it's the Prime Minister or the guy sleeping on the streets. And you judge people by their actions—*not* by their words or their position in life.

It means you walk confidently towards new challenges instead of backing off and making excuses. You're self-reliant, capable and confident, and refuse to live timidly. And you never take yourself too seriously.

Importantly, it's not about success or failure. It's simply about being true to yourself.

I know it sounds like a tough, almost impossible, standard to meet. And it is, because it needs to be.

Whatever else you do, don't try to fake it. If you need to get better, then do it. Just be yourself, and show everyone who you are and what you can do. Because in the end, that's all that really matters.

The Five Hardest Words To Live Up To.

Before I became an entrepreneur, I worked for a couple of very large companies. I did okay, but I wasn't a star by any means.

One day my boss pulled me aside and gave it to me straight.

"You're talented enough and smart enough to make it to the top. But you're not committed enough. Less talented blokes will always get the good jobs ahead of you unless you step up, engage yourself fully and show that you're serious. If we can't count on you then you won't make it. And that would be a terrible waste."

Two things were tripping me up back then: too low a care factor and a low activity level. And as I found out, that combination guaranteed mediocre career progress.

That was more than 20 years ago, but I've never forgotten the lesson. I was coasting along half-committed, and my career progress reflected it. I realised then and there that if I wanted to achieve something meaningful I needed to get serious.

A year later I left to start my first business. On day one I attached a small sign to my computer that read, "You can count on me." It was my promise to both me and my business, and it stayed there for ten years.

It turned out to be the greatest challenge of my business life. When I first put it up I didn't know how high the standard actually was. And while I'm far from perfect this ethos has helped guide my actions, and I do my best to live up to it every day.

But what does "You can count on me" actually mean? It means you can be counted on to produce a specific outcome, no matter what else is going on. You're dependable, and you keep your word. You stand behind your team, and always have their backs. You're fully engaged and committed—not a spectator.

Simply, you always do what you say you'll do.

Those five simple words—you can count on me—can change your fortune and propel you forward. Yes it's a high standard, and you have to work every day to live up to it. But the effort is certainly worth it.

Take up the challenge and see for yourself.

Understand Your True Net Worth

The concept of someone's 'net worth' is an interesting one. Some people will do a quick mental tally of their personal assets and liabilities to come up with a dollar figure. Others will grab their bank statements and mortgage documents, thump away on their calculator for a while, wonder whether they could actually sell their house for that much, and arrive at a number they quietly hope isn't too over-inflated.

But I don't think you can define someone's net worth simply by subtracting their liabilities from their assets. I believe a person's net worth is less about how much they've made and more about what they're made of.

The seemingly simple question, "What's most important to you?" is usually a good pointer to what people are made of. Most will answer automatically, blurting out "My family'. And for some that might be true.

But you can always get the real story by looking at where they *actually* spend their discretionary time and money. Does the family *really* get a fair allocation? Or is the time and money spent elsewhere? Words can lie, but behaviours never do.

So how do you increase your true net worth?

The key is to build the useful relationships you have both in number and in strength. It will help you get things done quickly, and contribute to the important things in your life.

In business they're the relationships that help you solve problems, exploit opportunities and ultimately get the job done. And in your personal life they're the people who matter to you and have got your back even on the darkest days.

In both situations you can't do without them, and the more you have the more you'll get done. But remember: these relationships are a two-way street. You don't build them by sinking the boot in when someone's down or running for the hills when things get uncomfortable. And you don't get them by finger pointing or claiming credit for the work of others.

Relationships like these are built by putting others first. By joining hands and fighting battles together. By being honest and transparent. By unequivocally supporting the people that matter to you. And by understanding your family and friends are the most precious assets you'll ever have.

As I said, net worth is less about how much you've made and more about what you're made of. It's far more complicated than just adding up assets and liabilities, but ultimately it's what net worth is *really* about.

Be Prepared To Get Your Hands Dirty

I got my first *real* job when I was 18, working in a paint factory 40 minutes away during the Christmas holidays. Starting at 6.30am I had to lug 44-gallon drums to a solvent filling station, don a safety mask and gloves, and fill the drums with an apparatus that resembled a garden hose. And once each drum was full I had to manhandle it out of the way and start filling the next one.

Once I filled 16 drums I'd put them on a heavy-duty trolley, wheel it to the nearby despatch area and hand-load a waiting truck. I'd load about five trucks every day, then sweep the factory floor and clean the toilets before heading home at 3pm.

And strangely, I enjoyed it.

I was the only university student working there. The rest of the employees were older men supporting families, and most of them had worked there for years.

To start with they pretty much ignored me other than to give me the worst jobs in the factory. Jobs they didn't want to do themselves. And believe me, some of them were terrible.

But no matter what job they gave me, I did it as fast and as well as I could. I also smiled a lot, and often asked if I could do more to help out. I didn't care what the job was—it made no difference to me. It was all dirty, hard, physical work that left me exhausted at the end of the day.

After a month their attitudes began to change. They started eating lunch with me, and sharing stories about their lives. They forgot I was a university student doing a holiday job, and so did I. I'd earned their respect because I worked hard and didn't complain.

The work didn't get any easier over the next two months. But I'd 'earned my stripes', and was now considered part of the team.

My enjoyment factor skyrocketed.

Experiences like these shape how you conduct yourself in business. The job was tough, but I made the most of it. Most jobs have good and bad parts. So what? They all need to be done. Why not by you?

When I was running companies it didn't matter if I had to take out the garbage or clinch a multi-million dollar deal. It was important to be a hard-working member of the team and lead by example. The best way to set an example is to do the tough tasks without complaining and then ask for more. It builds trust within teams and creates loyalty—valuable assets to call on when you need to.

Tough times aren't necessarily bad times. In fact, you can be having the time of your life. Three of us once fitted out six temporary retail stores in ten days. I can still see us lying on the floor of the last shop, eating pizza, drinking beer and laughing while replaying the events of the past few days. We were exhausted, happy, and proud of what we'd achieved.

Sometimes there's no choice but to dig deep to get something done. These are pivotal moments, when the true identity of a business is forged. Great businesses do *what* they have to do, *when* they have to do it. And the more often they do it, the more it becomes part of their DNA. When new people join the business they don't just *see* this attitude, they *feel* it. Which in turn influences how they behave and perform.

In hindsight, I've always loved the hard times. To me there's nothing better than being backed into a corner and having to fight your way out. Not only do you learn about yourself and your team, you also create the legends you'll remember fondly in your old age.

Stubborn Or Persistent?

There's no future in being stubborn. And yet persistence is a highly prized attribute. So what's the difference between the two? (Yes, there *is* a difference. Stubbornness is not persistence.)

Stubborn people keep doing the same things even when overwhelming evidence suggests they should stop. It's like banging your head against a wall that won't break. There's no future in it, and you certainly won't achieve your goals. It's better to quit when you think you can still succeed and either change direction or make new plans.

Some people subscribe to the idea they should 'never give in.' While it's a romantic notion, a slightly amended approach might be more practical. In my view it's actually better to give in, on occasions, if it will put you in a stronger future position. Winning every battle might feel good, but sometimes you need to retreat to win the war.

Adapting the idea to 'never give in *easily*' might better describe how persistent you should be. But what does it mean in practice?

It means you have to remain open-minded to sound arguments, even when you'd rather ignore them and keep doing what you're doing. You need to be prepared to admit mistakes, learn from them, and move on quickly.

But you also need grittiness, and a determination to succeed. Never take no for an answer unless it's obviously a lost cause, and always be prepared to make that last call or arrange that last meeting 'just in case.'

And *never* give in easily.

The line between persistence and stubbornness can blur at times, and may only be obvious in hindsight. The trick is to keep a clear head, persist, and be relentless about only doing things that contribute to your longer-term objectives.

And if you do it honestly and diligently, it should knock any stubbornness out of you.

Don't Let Anyone Else Tell You What You Are Worth

I wasn't exactly a model student at school. My heightened sense of larrikinism and desire to constantly 'entertain' my classmates made me quite disruptive and I got into trouble a lot.

Which is why I spent all of Grade 12 studying History from the library. I wasn't allowed to attend class, and was given no hope of passing the HSC exam.

In the end not only did I pass, I actually got a higher score than many of my classmates.

I now realise what motivated me: my teacher writing me off. I deserved the punishment, and didn't even mind working from the library. But even as a 17-year-old, being expected to fail was unacceptable.

It was a cataclysmic motivator for me, and I subconsciously decided never to conform to anyone else's view of me.

When I was young I rebelled with bad behaviour. But as I grew older, and especially when I got into my own businesses, it became a gritty determination to push through painful situations and work harder than everyone else. I was looking for ways to do things differently, and carve out my own path in the process.

It's still a work in progress, and success and failure have come in equal measures. But each day I get up happy, committed, motivated and ready to go again.

What keeps me motivated?

Firstly, the naysayers, critics, and sceptics keen to point out what's wrong but unable to come up with a better way. People who throw up problems without offering any solutions annoy me. We all have a greater responsibility than that. It's easy to come up with a million seemingly sensible reasons why something might not work. The skill is in finding the one reason it might, and that's what I focus on.

Secondly, my fascination with possibilities for the future. I don't know what the world will be like in 2030 or 2050. What I *do* know is that contributing to its development is our responsibility, and we need to start now. But we can only do that through kindness, innovation, good business ethics, a focus on learning, and a willingness to smash through barriers we think are impossible to break through right now.

I'm not sure what I can contribute (if anything), but I'm definitely going to find out.

Be Curious

In 2013 I took my family, including my two young sons, to Borneo for a holiday. It wasn't luxurious (some of our accommodation would barely rate half a star), and we did some pretty rough traveling at times. We got rained on regularly, ate some pretty average food (especially in the local villages), and had a run in with leeches during a particularly soggy jungle trek. We even returned to our jungle hut one afternoon to find a couple of macaque monkeys had taken up residence.

So what's the payoff for doing a trip like this?

The priceless experiences.

We saw orang-utans and proboscis monkeys in the wild, elephants bathing in the river, and giant sea turtles swimming near our boat. We played soccer and volleyball with local villagers before staying overnight in their homes. We trekked through pristine jungles and visited Snake Island inhabited by thousands of sea snakes.

Some of my friends said things like, "You guys are really adventurous" and "We could never do that type of trip". All I could think was, "Why not?" Sure it wasn't a hotel in Bali or an apartment in Surfers Paradise. But you'll never experience wonders like these lying around a pool or going shopping.

And I don't know if 'adventurous' is the best way to describe it. 'Curious' would probably be more accurate. It could explain why I trekked to the Everest Base Camp (on a whim 20-odd years ago), took up water skiing last year, or recently became a basketball coach despite the fact I'd never coached or even played the game before.

It's the reason I'm writing this book, and no doubt why I've started so many businesses in the past 20 years.

What I *do* know is that I don't enjoy the status quo. I need to find out what *else* is out there—what else I can learn, experience and contribute.

And I suspect a lot of other people feel the same way.

Of course, thinking about it is one thing. Actually doing something about it means dealing with the unknown (and the fear associated with it), which can shut down our innate curiosity and lead to inertia, perpetuating the status quo.

And that's a big problem.

Overcoming apathy and inertia means be curious and, more importantly, relatively fearless. But it's worth the effort. It can get you out of a rut, open up life-changing experiences, and take you on a journey of self-discovery.

Whether it takes you to Borneo or not doesn't matter. What counts is getting off the treadmill of routine, complacency and fear.

Find Time To Think

I can't recall the last time a really good idea came to me when I was sitting in my office trying to think one up. It's never happened. It's usually because I'm too focused on getting things done or dealing with interruptions or trying to meet a deadline.

Instead I'll get my best ideas while I'm driving, taking a shower, going for a walk, traveling or while reading a book. It always happens when I'm relaxed and my mind is blank. I'm not trying to solve problems or deal with pressing issues.

And all of a sudden a really good idea will just pop into my head.

The lesson for me is that I need to take *time out* to think, read, observe or ponder. I can't do that with other people around either. I need to fully relax and let my mind wander. It helps when I visit somewhere new or try a new experience as this seems to get my creative juices flowing.

I remembering reading that Bill Gates would go off the grid for one week twice a year to read. He did it for over 20 years. Alone. Everyone, even family, were banned from contacting him. He called it his 'Think Weeks' and spent up to 20 hours every day reading and pondering internal Microsoft documents. No topics were out of bounds and he used this time to consider the future direction of Microsoft. Many ground-breaking ideas and strategies came to him during his Think Weeks.

Like Gates, the great US President, Teddy Roosevelt, was a voracious reader. He didn't just read books, he devoured them. While he was President he would read a book every day before breakfast and another one or two every night. He read tens of thousands of books during his lifetime, including hundreds in foreign languages.

He was an expert speed reader, able to retain huge amounts of information that he used during his life. As a result of his encyclopaedic knowledge he made quick connections and built great rapport with people everywhere and this had a major impact on his leadership and influence.

It's important to create 'quiet time' regularly to ponder the future. Let your mind wander and roam. Finding an hour or day or even an hour a week is enough to get started. This will spark your imagination and new ideas will start flooding in.

Start by reading more. One non-fiction book per month is a good starting target. Blogs are good too. Subscribe to some that interest you and participate in the forums.

But if you want to do more, challenge yourself to write down one new idea every week – work it through from conception to implementation. It doesn't matter whether you implement it or not. What is important is the discipline and regularity in doing it. Soon enough, you'll get good at it and a great idea will emerge that may change your life.

The Odds Of Success

A few years ago at a seminar I heard some startling statistics about the likelihood you will achieve financial successful in your life by the age of 65:

- One person will be wealthy.
- Four more will be financially independent.
- Fifteen will still be working full time.
- Another thirty five or so will be flat broke.
- The remainder will be making ends meet through part time work and pension payments.

Interesting statistics.

I think most of us would like to be financially independent by the time we reach 65 (or at least be close to it). We'd also like to choose whether we work or not. And relying on a pension to fund our retirement is unlikely to be anyone's ideal way to spend their golden years.

But why does it happen?

I think people just get *stuck*. Stuck in repetitive patterns of behaviour that produces the exact same results every time. The outcome is predictable because the behaviour is predictable. And this causes, in so many cases, for people to fall short of their dreams and aspirations. Some do a bit better and have moderate success. But only a minority of people 'behave' successfully and become successful.

There's no doubt it's just easier and more convenient to conform. Keep your head down and try and fit in. Get on the treadmill and keep pedalling. Don't rock the boat. Stay in your comfort zone and keep doing what you've always done.

Get up. Go to work. Come home. Have dinner. Watch TV. Go to bed. Dine out every week or two. Take a holiday once a year. Then repeat this cycle year in, year out.

It's not a bad life.

But it will produce predictable results that you may not like.

If you want more than this, you'll need to do more. And it's not just about working hard either (although that is important). It's about working smart too.

And taking risks and making your own luck.

In my experience, the people that achieve success are usually not the smartest or most talented people around. But they are hugely determined. At every stage they have forced themselves to do things that were uncomfortable and scary. They stepped into the unknown, sucked up their fear and focused on making the best possible decisions, every time. Along the way they learnt new skills, overcame their weaknesses and expanded their capabilities.

But how do you get started?

First: Find a major purpose in your life. What do you want to achieve? Look for challenges that stimulate you and you're passionate about.

Can you write your major purpose in a sentence or two?

Steve Jobs wanted to leave a dent in the universe. Martin Luther King wanted to create equality for black people. It doesn't have to be as grand as that. But it does need to be important (and worthwhile).

Richard Branson came at it from a different angle but it is equally powerful, especially in the context of his life story - "To have fun in my journey through life and learn from mistakes."

Mine is that I want to push myself to do hard, difficult things. To find out how much I am capable of. To never stop learning and to never *settle* for 'good enough' in my life.

What is yours?

If it is not immediately obvious, then spend some time figuring it out. It will eventually come to you.

Second: take risks to achieve your major purpose. Many people start something, but few finish it. Be resilient. Don't quit. Your major purpose won't be easy. You will hit problems and suffer set-backs. They're temporary. Keep going. Fail your way to success through sheer bloody-mindedness, if need be.

Those who succeed are those who endure.

Third: keep the faith. Passionate people attract others. Tell your story. Live and breathe it. Don't listen to people who try to put you or your ideas down. Believe in yourself and sooner or later others will believe in you too.

Without passion it will be hard to start and even harder to keep going, especially when the times get tough (and they will). You can't do that unless you're 100% committed and engaged. And if you don't love what you're doing then it will be no fun and any passion you have will dissipate quickly.

Finally: audit your progress annually. Measure your forward progress and satisfaction levels. I do this because I don't want to perpetuate things that make me unhappy or disillusioned. It helps me to avoid missing opportunities or heading down the wrong road. It's highly cathartic and it has kept my life on track.

It also forces me to ask these two hard questions - Am I happy? Am I living the life I want?

While sometimes difficult, I always try to answer honestly. Then I tune things up and move forward again.

Perhaps Mark Twain summed it up best when he said - "twenty years from now you will be more disappointed by the things that you didn't do than by the ones you did. So throw off the bowlines. Sail away from the safe harbour. Catch the trade winds in your sails. Explore. Dream. Discover."

There are boundless opportunities out there. But they only come to the people who actually go looking for them.

Will you be one of them?

Ethical Business

Honesty and integrity are a vital part of any successful business. You may be able to cheat a customer, or other stakeholder, once but you'll never be able to do it again. And not only could you lose that relationship but you could also damage your business permanently.

It simply isn't worth it.

So be honest, act with integrity, and always fulfil your promises.

.

Do Business Ethically

It always amuses me when someone feels the need to tell me they're honest, trustworthy, and a person of their word. It's even worse when they use phrases like "To be completely honest with you" (What, you weren't before?) or "You can trust me, I'm a fair guy".

These 'assurances' rarely fill me with confidence. In fact, they usually arouse suspicion because if what the person said was actually true, they wouldn't need to say it.

A person's actions mean far more to me than their words. Which is why ethics and integrity are so important in business.

I remember reading *The Power of Ethical Management* by Ken Blanchard and Norman Vincent Peale, which provided a three-point ethics checklist you can apply to any decision you make:

- Is it legal?
- Is it balanced?
- How will it make me feel about myself?

These three questions cut through the noise and grey areas, and really get to the heart of ethical behaviour.

- **Is it legal?** This may seem like a pretty straightforward question, but it's about more than just breaking the law. It's also about needing to operate within agreed company policy, and not doing anything that's improper, illegal, immoral, or that could harm or embarrass the company.

And if you can't answer yes to *this* question, there's no point even considering the other two.

- **Is it balanced?** Or, more importantly, is it fair? Actions that result in one party winning big and the other losing big invariably cause problems later, especially if it happens regularly. It's better to ensure both parties get something out of the deal.

  This doesn't mean you can't be tough, negotiate hard and demand superior performance from everyone you deal with. You can and you should. But you need to leave some 'meat on the bone' for those relationships that are important to you now, or could be in the future.

  Because if those relationships don't prosper, there's a good chance you won't either.

- **How will it make me feel about myself?** Would I be proud or ashamed? Would I tell my parents, spouse or kids about it without sugar-coating the facts? Would I like to see it on the evening news?

Getting three yeses may be a tough assignment, but it's a fabulous way to do business. Ethical businesses do better and last longer than unethical businesses, which should be reason enough to act ethically. Unfortunately some businesses prefer to take a less ethical path, perhaps looking for a shortcut to success.

But you can't undo history. And while you may think everyone's forgotten about an unethical action you took years ago, chances are *someone* out there will remember (regulators, competitors, suppliers, staff, etc.) Just pray they don't have the means and the will to hold you accountable for it in the future.

There's Nothing Wrong With 'Old School' Business

In some respects I'm from the old school of business, and I'm not ashamed to admit it. I like agreements to be in writing, and I expect everyone to live up to what they've agreed to do. If I screw up, then I make a commitment to fix the problem quickly, no matter how expensive, embarrassing or inconvenient it might be. And I expect the other party to do the same.

This simple approach puts a high importance on setting clear expectations up front. That's not always easy to do, but it is possible. And you get better at it the more times you do it.

If you're constantly arguing with partners, suppliers, customers and staff about what you expected vs. what they delivered, then a little old-school business might be just the ticket you need.

To mitigate potential problems it's important to spend time early on making sure all joint expectations are understood and agreed to. Labour the point if you need to, but never rush into a new agreement until the fundamentals are clear and everybody understands them. Then put it in writing. Nobody can argue they didn't understand what they were signing if you take your time and work through it point by point.

This approach works for me because I'm time poor and hate re-writing deals after the event. By setting clear expectations in advance, and then discussing what will happen if things go wrong, we end up with fewer surprises. And if things *do* go wrong, you need to be empathetic and open to resolution options. But you should never feel obliged to go back on a deal if you didn't create the problem.

Of course, it only works if you behave the same way when you screw up. It sets a behavioural precedent that's hard to argue against. It's not about winning or losing. It is about accountability. Do what you say you'll do, but if it goes wrong then fix it quickly and make it whole again. If you don't, the trust you've built will be eroded and they may even question your sincerity. And that's bad business on every level.

Yes I'm old school, and unashamedly so. I've learnt the hard way that an extra hour or two of good preparation that's embodied in a written agreement will save a lot of time fixing problems later on. Time I'd rather spend working on the next opportunity.

Just Tell The Truth

I get annoyed when I'm lied to.

When I was running Calendar Club back in the 1990s, I noticed our key retail competitors were all consistently selling at 25% off the recommended retail prices. For a while I assumed they were funding the margin reduction themselves to significantly increase sales with the lower prices.

This discounting strategy continued for years, and began to have an impact on Calendar Club's sales.

I understood the economics of the marketplace, and couldn't work out how they could keep it up for so long without going broke or stopping. I asked one of our main suppliers several times whether our competitors received any specific trading terms encouraging them to discount.

Each time I was told, "No".

One day the company's sales manager called in to our office for a chat. At one point he dropped a pile of files on the floor, and I helped him pick them up. Unfortunately for him, he left one of his files behind after our meeting.

The *Independent Retailers Discount Program* contained a detailed strategy of how to *encourage* independent retailers to discount their calendars by 25% to combat Calendar Club's market dominance.

The following week I had another meeting with the sales director, and once again I asked if any discounting programs were in place. When he said "No", I produced the file and asked whether it belonged to him.

Caught out, he had no option but to start being honest.

There's nothing worse dealing with someone who's looking you in the eye while lying through their teeth. Why do people do it? To protect their own self-interest and cover something up—a mistake, an inadequacy, an oversight, or in our case an inconvenient truth. And instead of passing on the bad news, they try to bury it and hope it goes away.

Continual dishonesty will damage your reputation—permanently. Nobody wants to buy from people or companies who behave like this.

On the other hand, studies show people buy more often from companies and sales people they trust. So it's easy to see that honesty is the best approach. Even if things go wrong occasionally, customers are more likely to forgive you and give you another chance if you're honest.

And when during the bad times, this could end up being the key to your survival.

The same goes for your vendors and staff as well. They help determine whether or not you can keep your promise to your customers, and so they need to live up to the same ethical standards.

Just tell the truth. It's a simple, unambiguous rule that's critical for a long and successful business career.

Apologise But Mean It!

No matter how hard you try, sometimes things go wrong that affect other people. They may feel let down, angry, even hostile. But above all they'll want answers.

This is a pivotal moment in any relationship, and how you respond could well determine whether it continues or dies.

A long-standing supplier to a business I was associated with screwed up. And I mean *really* screwed up. They let us down badly on what they'd promised, which was a huge inconvenience and cost us money.

It could have been the end of the relationship. But 12 months on it's never been better.

Why? Because the CEO got personally involved, making both a sincere, heartfelt apology and a genuine commitment to fix the problem quickly.

We just *had* to give them another chance. I can still recall his words: "We screwed up badly, and we're deeply embarrassed. More than anything we're really sorry, and I will personally fix this problem and give you my assurance that it won't happen again."

And he did. One hundred percent.

I admire people who can apologise authentically like this. It's not easy to do, and you have to lay yourself bare to do it. You can't make excuses, or provide a list of mitigating circumstances, or use the word "But". Instead you have to accept responsibility and say, "I screwed up and I'm really sorry. Please forgive me and give me another chance. I won't let you down again."

And then make sure you don't.

An honest apology:

- explains what happened and why—without excuses or blame
- acknowledges the pain that's been caused
- describes what will be done to ensure it never happens again
- includes a genuine request for forgiveness.

Most of all, you need to apologise as soon as you screwed up, miss a deadline or receive a customer complaint.

An honest, unconditional apology is a powerful statement, and says a lot about you and your organisation, and what you stand for. Yes, it can be painful. But if you want to endure and prosper in business, you need to know when—and how—to do it.

The Ethics Dilemma

Back in the late 1980s I was standing on the sideline watching a game of rugby between two arch-rivals. One team had dominated the other for more than two years, but this match was close with a real chance of an upset.

With a couple of minutes to go, one of the wingers broke free and was heading for the try line. Only the fullback stood between him and victory. As he swerved and side-stepped to evade the fullback he got clipped, momentarily lost his balance, and then regained it to go over in the corner for the match-winning try.

But instead of celebrating, he walked back to confer with the touch judge. After remonstrating for a moment or so, the try was reversed and a line out ordered. He'd put his foot on the sideline, and in rugby that's out. No try. The match was lost.

The touch judge, who'd slipped on the heavy, muddy ground trying to keep up, had missed it. But the player hadn't—he knew he was out.

After the match ended, a few people in the crowd started clapping. Then others joined in. Pretty soon everyone, including the referee and the other team, was clapping the team and the player involved. It was a remarkable moment.

The player didn't want to win unfairly. And in the end, neither did his team. They wanted to win honestly and without excuses. After two more attempts they managed to beat the other team, and the victory was so much sweeter because it was legitimate and hard-earned.

In the scheme of things it wasn't a big game—there were only 150 people or so watching it. But the memory has stuck with me.

In our world of drug cheats, performance-enhancing drugs, pushy parents and 'half-honest' executives, too many people are prepared to cross that line. To claim victory they don't deserve, and sacrifice their personal integrity as if it was nothing.

But victory doesn't come cheap. It never has, and it never will. Ben Johnson, Marion Jones, Lance Armstrong and others have learnt that lesson the hard way.

If it comes down to a single moment when you know you've put your foot on the sideline, but no-one else will know, do you put your hand up or keep it down?

It's your call. What happens next?

Finding and Creating Opportunities

As the saying goes, "Opportunity knocks only once". Unfortunately, some people are still sitting around, waiting for that knock. These days you have to find or create your own.

The good news is they're everywhere. You just need to know how to find/create them, and then not let them slip away.

The Best Opportunities Are Always Found In the Same Two Places

How many times have you heard someone say they want to set up their own business but don't know where to start? Or that they can't find any opportunities and don't know how to create one themselves?

Unfortunately, there's a good chance they will never set up their own business. Not because they don't have the resources or the talent, but because they're looking for ready-made opportunities served up on a plate.

And that will never happen. The competition for opportunities is too intense, and there are usually other people around with far greater resources to exploit the more obvious ones.

To launch and/or exploit an opportunity and embed it in the marketplace, the budding entrepreneur or business builder needs to work faster and smarter than ever before. And they need to find a narrow but potentially deep niche their competitors have either ignored or not yet discovered.

Which leads inevitably to two places where all the best opportunities are—sectors or niches where customers are being either:

- over-charged; and/or
- under-served.

And the very best of them may well intersect the two.

Think about it. Any great business has exploited one of these circumstances. Or both.

Richard Branson targeted old, complacent industries (e.g. airlines, rail etc) with poor service records and provided a market alternative that did exactly the opposite.

Air BnB and Uber unlocked 'dormant' or under-utilised assets, lowered costs, created a unique customer experience and disrupted the hotel and taxi industry in the process.

In my own experience, Calendar Club provided huge product choice, previously unavailable, to an under-served market. E-pay disrupted a sector used to physical cards for mobile phone top-ups (which were hated by retailers) and through technology provided a service delivery model that was irresistible to customers. And Powershop, with its low cost operating model, capitalised on the general hostility towards electricity retailers by cutting prices and providing a much enhanced customer experience through its online consumption tools and the best service in the industry.

Opportunities are everywhere. Many of them are right under our noses. Think about all those products and services that make your life easier, simpler and better. That have saved you time, money and hassle. And made you more productive.

Here are some of my current favourites that fit into this category:

- Westfield's red/green light parking system in some of their shopping centres. Instead of driving round and round looking for a car spot you just look for a green light and head straight to the vacant spot. Love it!
- Getting the groceries home delivered.
- My ironing man. Putting my crinkled shirts in a basket at the front door and 24 hours later they

reappear miraculously on hangers, crisply pressed, for the bargain price of $2 each. Magnificent!
- Getting the lawn mowed every fortnight for $20 and rarely seeing the guy who does it.
- The Do Not Call Register. Tele-marketers be gone!
- The (ATM-like) check-in kiosks at the airport meaning I can arrive at the airport later, check-in faster and still catch my flight. (Note to self - why can't we do this at hotels?)
- My (occasional) overseas Virtual Assistant – when time is tight, call the Philippines!

I get a kick out of each of these things.

On the flipside I hate stuff that complicates my life or is unnecessary. Paying rapacious by-the-hour rates for Wi-Fi internet at hotels falls into this category. Likewise, waiting around in a 'four hour window' for a tradesman or technician to show up. Four hours, really?

All the stuff mentioned above is small and seemingly inconsequential but each improves your life, even if just a little bit. They reduce time, pain and don't cost much - some cost nothing.

But what each gives you is more time to do more important things and that is priceless. And within each of these products or services a smart entrepreneur or business builder has uncovered a need, unlocked an opportunity and worked hard to commercialise a product.

There is a lesson here. And that is to be constantly picking apart the micro-details of each interaction with a customer (in any sector) and be constantly looking for ways to remove *pain* and make their lives a bit easier. If you adopt this approach you will find new opportunities everywhere.

It's impossible to do this from the ivory tower or the conference room, however. And in many cases customers don't really know what they want, or can't articulate it well, until they see it. Henry Ford famously said that "if I had asked my customers what they wanted they would have said a faster horse."

Instead you have to walk in their shoes, understand their true underlying (unarticulated) needs, aspirations AND the rhythms of their lives to understand the problems that matter to them and then map solutions back to solving them.

These days whenever I have a good (significant) idea I try to talk to at least 50 people and elicit feedback about what I'm doing. I don't speak to them when I'm unprepared either. I usually have a basic prototype 'built' that I can show them. Giving them the ability to 'play' with a prototype results in more useful feedback because they can better visualise what I'm talking about and trying to do.

I'm also interested in more than just their verbal response. I watch closely how they physically *handle* the prototype and what their instinctive first reactions are. Essentially I'm looking for patterns of behaviour which will emerge and evolve out of *all* the feedback of each of the people I talk to.

Doing this 50 times is hard work. It can become repetitive but is the quickest way I know to do grass roots market research. It's amazingly effective too. It's also much better than trying to second guess what you can so easily find out.

The Internet has been a great help in finding and exploiting market opportunities. It's given large and small local businesses access to a global marketplace *and*, in many cases, reduced their supply chain costs by letting them sell directly to their customers. Customers have also embraced it because the cost savings are being passed on to them in the form of lower prices. It's a win-win situation, with the only losers being the incumbent suppliers operating with traditional business models and needing to sell at higher prices.

These days the best opportunities lie beyond the familiar, and they're never obvious until someone puts one on the ground in a marketplace. But that's the skill. Find it first, and you might be the business that changes the game.That's the game of opportunity identification and creation.

Creating Something Valuable

My first attempt at creating something valuable (or at least would give me some much-needed pocket money) was the lawn mowing business I started when I was 17. I didn't have a clue what was I doing. But I *did* know I needed customers. So I hand-wrote flyers and walked the streets dropping them into local mailboxes. Eventually I upgraded my marketing efforts to a small ad in the local newspaper.

I made it clear I didn't own a lawn mower, which was a small disadvantage. But I still managed to get lots of work because I charged $6 per hour instead of the $10 my 'competitors' were charging. Pretty soon I was working 5 days a week and I even had to recruit one of my best mates to handle my work overflow.

It was a great way to make fast money in my school holidays. And I learned a valuable lesson. Whether or not I owned a lawn mower didn't matter as long as I was reliable, cheap and did a good job.

In the 30-odd years since, here's what else I've learnt about creating valuable businesses:

- **Do something you love.** This is very important. Treat it as your life's work, and care for it as if it was part of your family. Passion will sustain you when times get tough—and they will.
- **Solve a real market problem.** The harder the problem the better. To do that, ask and then answer these three questions:
  - Where are the inefficiencies in the market?
  - Where are customers being overcharged or under-served?
  - Where are the competitors vulnerable?
- **Don't force people to change their behaviours unnecessarily.** Ingrained behaviours are very hard to break. Instead, focus on making their lives better in some way without hassling them or making them jump through hoops. If you make it easy and simple for them to buy, the chances of them doing so increase dramatically.
- **Be hard to copy.** This will protect you. You need to be different because 'me-too' businesses are vulnerable and replaceable in a competitive marketplace.
- **Avoid going head-to-head with big market players on their turf.** There's no glory in getting squashed by an elephant. Instead, play in a space that's hard for them to access and always be hard to catch.

- **Do it as if your life depended on it.** This requires passion, boundless energy, discipline, doggedness and a great team to support you.
- **Don't talk about money or your exit strategy.** It's boring and indulgent. Just focus on building something great and doing the hard yards to commercialise it. This should keep you occupied. And as long as you make the right moves, the money will eventually follow.
- **Have enough capital (or access to it) to last at least a year.** Running out of money is an inglorious way to end your dream.

Ultimately, you're looking for niches (or micro-niches) that have been missed, ignored, neglected or under-developed by the rest of the market. While the niche may be narrow (from a product perspective) it must have a large pool of potential customers you can tap into that's prepared to pay a fair price for what you are offering. As I have said previously the best place to find these niches is in sectors where customers are currently being underserved and/or overcharged.

Identifying these niches is only the first stage. You then need to exploit them by being better and/or cheaper than what's currently available in the market.

This is not an easy thing to do. But don't let this deter you. Value is only created when difficult and complex problems are solved (at scale) in ways that significantly enhance people's lives.

The Days Of 'Sustainable' Competitive Advantage Are Over

The smartphone is a great example of how technology can render traditional business sectors obsolete, or at least make them pivot quickly to avoid terminal decline.

Just think of everything you do with your smartphone and how you had to do them before. On any given day I'll:

- use the satellite navigation tool
- surf the 'net
- download email
- take a couple of photos
- read some media articles
- scan a document and email it
- use a flashlight app
- check my heart rate
- play a game
- pay a few bills
- send a handful of text messages
- make a few phone calls
- set the alarm to wake up
- write some notes
- do some basic calculations
- listen to some music

And to most people I'm just a novice user.

I now manage a decent chunk of my life with a small device I keep in my pocket. That certainly wasn't the case a few years ago.

But it was an easy choice to make. In most cases the 'old' solutions were more difficult, less efficient and more costly. Each change I made was incremental, and I slowly adopted them one by one. Cumulatively they've

65

improved my efficiency and, most importantly, saved me time.

But what about the wider implications? Aggregating these tools and utilities into a single device has created/ changed/decimated entire industries—the postal service and banks, digital designers and the media sector, and of course the camera, printer, scanner and 'dumb' phone makers. They've all either benefited or been adversely affected by the functionality now available in these technological wonders.

The idea of having a **sustainable** competitive advantage, once lauded as the holy grail of business, is now totally unrealistic. Today's competitive advantage is transient at best, and assuming a market sector will remain stable is a poor assumption. Markets shift regularly, with most of the changes being too small to notice. But eventually these small changes accumulate to create industry-wide circumstances that will either trouble or please you, depending on whether you're prepared for them.

Businesses like Blockbuster, Borders, Nokia, Motorola and Kodak learnt this lesson the hard way. After holding positions of market leadership for years (if not decades) they are now either on their last legs or gone altogether.

They failed because they became irrelevant in the marketplace, and their customers chose to buy better offers elsewhere. It didn't happen overnight. But neither did the rise of their competitors (Netflix, Amazon, Samsung and Apple) who ultimately destroyed them with better products, cutting edge business models and superior service delivery methods.

I've always wondered why the incumbents didn't act sooner and make the necessary changes to protect themselves? Why did they just sit back and let these upstarts grow and eventually usurp them? Why didn't they use their significant resources to develop and implement the 'next big thing' themselves?

The answer is simple (and cautionary). Because it's hard to pivot when you're managing a business that's going well. And it's even harder to spend money on activities that could cannibalise your profitable core business in the future.

It feels a lot more comfortable to just keep your head down and keep the gravy train moving, making small incremental improvements to your product offerings, believing your position is unassailable and that the market minnows will fail.

They were probably also not helped by several common *scourges* that are prevalent in many businesses, large and small:

- The heavy skewing of remuneration and incentives to achieving short term results.
- An overweight focus on analytical thinking – i.e. proving it by the numbers.
- Too many questions like – will it work? Or, can you *guarantee* its success?
- A general fear of looking bad – i.e. failing and/or making mistakes.
- No democracy in ideas generation – i.e. all ideas flow down from the top.
- Relying too heavily on the past to make predictions about the future.

All of these situations discourage trying new approaches and ideas. And, even if changes are made, they are usually safe and small in nature. Without a willingness to (sometimes) climb out on a limb and experiment (without knowing the answers in advance) the only possible outcome is that the status quo is maintained.

Unfortunately, more often than not, this approach eventually runs out of steam. And doing it for too long has led to the demise of companies large and small.

It is important to remember that customers don't care if your current methods make you money, or how much it will cost you to pivot and head in a new direction. All they want is a solution that's 'better, cheaper and faster' than what's available now.

And they'll support any company that can give it to them.

So what's the answer?

First, stop worrying about being the biggest or even the best. Those days are over.

The same applies to the notion of industry best practice – why not break new ground rather than model yourself on a so-called *expert's opinion* of the world?

What is most important is to be different and unique, because that's what makes you attractive to the market. And keep asking yourself this question - how can I solve this problem in a different way to what the market is used to?

Second, realise that sectors with inefficiency, waste, AND good margins will be irresistible to new entrants, especially if the entry barriers are low. The good players will remove the waste, keep the margins (or most of it) and improve the customer experience. It's a winning combination that's hard to beat.

Third, be really good at one thing, and *only* one. Then discard everything—products, customers, even staff—that doesn't help you deliver it.

Finally, understand that the value of long-term operational strategies is questionable. The key is to remain nimble so you can react quickly to risks and opportunities as they emerge.

The one thing that protects businesses in the long run is constant innovation. Yes, that term is being used far too often these days. But it *is* the fuel for change, and building internal innovation capability that sits at the core of organisational decisions is fundamental to success.

When it's done properly, innovation addresses real market problems by discovering what customers *really* want and what they're prepared to pay for. And the only way to learn, develop and successfully commercialise it is through relentless in-market experimentation, improvisation, and good old trial and error.

Mind you, asking the right questions can help a lot. Here are two of the most critical (in my view, at least):

- How do I get my product/ service into my customers' hands in the quickest, most efficient way possible?
- How can I compel them to buy from me?

Spending time, effort and resources imagining the future and anticipating what customers will respond to favourably in the next 2-5 years is a sensible strategy. It's extremely challenging to think in this way, however, and you can't do it with both feet stuck in the past, or by focusing on protecting your legacy business.

You also have to do more than just optimise your current business model. You may need to invest in new business models well before it feels comfortable, even if it means cannibalising your current business. As an example, don't wait for the sales of a product or service to mature or decline prior to introducing a modified version into the market.

Here is a challenge that I have set some of the teams I have worked with – within 12-24 months have 10% (or 5% or 20%) of your revenue coming from products or services that do not exist today.

This might seem daunting and it is intended to be. It motivates people to start thinking creatively and forces the business leaders to make innovation a priority.

Some businesses achieved less than 10% and some a lot more but in almost every case it forced positive change. Almost all are better off as a result – not just financially but culturally as well.

While nothing is certain, this approach will provide strong protection no matter how disruptive (or seemingly stable) a sector is.

The other option is to do nothing: deny that the market is changing, and keep pumping out the same old products and services every year. Which works well— until it doesn't.

It's a fine balance. But ultimately it's the only way to stay relevant and important to your customers.

And in hindsight I'm sure the former chiefs of Blockbuster, Borders, Kodak and those other fallen companies would agree with me.

Stop Planning, And Start Doing

In the mid-1990s, when I first ventured out into the entrepreneurial world, the Internet barely existed. If you wanted to learn something you read the newspaper, watched TV, visited the library or bookstore, or talked to people who knew more about it.

Business moved at a slower pace back then, which gave you more protection and let you plan your business using more traditional, deliberate methods. You could spend months deliberating how to launch something new, refining your plan to the point of perfection, doing several prototypes, running focus groups, doing test marketing, getting a proof of concept ready and then *finally* launching.

These days you simply can't do that. With websites such as trendwatching.com alerting people about new trends every day, and vast amounts of information just a Google search away, you have no choice but to move faster.

Consequently, the time to conceive and launch anything (e.g. new business, new idea, new business model) has been dramatically reduced. The old 'Ready, Aim, Fire' approach has changed to 'Ready, Fire, Iterate, Fire, Iterate, Fire'.

But while the planning phase has been truncated, it still needs to be rock solid and incorporate a fluid approach that learns and adjusts from market feedback. That's why getting into the market as early as possible is so important. Only then will you see the flaws and imperfections of your plan, and be able to do something about it.

From my experience, four common assumptions are 'implicit' in most organisational business plans:

1. We're solving a market problem that needs to be solved
2. The market will reward us for solving it by buying our products
3. We can get a fair/good price for what we're selling
4. Our competitors will respond rationally

Unfortunately, you won't know whether your assumptions are true until you push your offer into the market. Speculation is far less valuable than actually finding out.

Whether your next competitor is a kid sitting on a beanbag with a laptop or a fast-moving industry behemoth hungry for new growth prospects, one thing is clear: they may well be eyeing off the same opportunity you are. And the only way you can get there first is to stop planning and start doing.

Managing Risk

Understanding and managing risk is a key part of being successful in business. You have to ask the right questions, test every assumption, and look beyond the numbers. It's a subtle blend of art and science overlaid with a willingness to push the boundaries when you need to.

The Least-Questioned Assumptions Are Often The Most Dangerous

Looking back on some of the failures (big and small) in my career, I can almost invariably track their cause back to one single theme—letting faulty assumptions slip through unchecked, untested, or just blindly accepted. It usually happened when someone passionately believed they were right, and convinced me and others their assumptions were correct. Mind you, when I was younger I was, at times, the one doing the convincing.

The failure was mostly due to being overly optimistic about what was possible. Yes, it's important to dream big. But you can't have your plans imploding because you overstated your assumptions by a factor of five.

Nowadays I'm a bit older and hopefully wiser, and don't get too caught up in the hype and emotion any more. I've lost money from believing in the 'next big thing' and so now I'm far more realistic, even slightly cynical. My brow starts furrowing when I'm within a kilometre of anything that sounds fanciful or too good to be true.

I'm particularly suspicious of:

- Industry minnows that base their sales pitch on claiming their competitors are hopeless, outdated and have inferior business models. Try selling your specific benefits, pal.
- Johnny-come-lately types who immediately criticise everything and claim they have all the answers after a week in charge. 'Saviours' are (usually) dangerous.
- Business plans with big hockey stick curves in the future. It doesn't happen often.

- Assumptions based on statistics or experiences from other countries. Iceland, you say?
- Statements like, "Even if we only get five percent of the market we'll have a great business". Duh.
- Businesses that will crumble if favourable government legislation changes overnight. Governments *do* change their mind.
- Frontal assaults on entrenched market players. Try stealth—you might last longer.
- Teams that have no 'skin in the game'. Money motivates.

When I test assumptions, I stick to tried and true fundamentals:

1. What market problem are you trying to solve?
2. Is it worth solving? Why?
3. Why do you think *you* can solve it?
4. How will you make money from solving it?
5. Will you make enough money to justify your efforts and investment?

What these questions do is expedite a long-winded interrogation of assumptions, and find out whether the business is actually focused on solving a *real* market problem at the lowest possible cost.

Any assumptions should be tied to these questions, and then thrashed to within an inch of their lives. If you still have a viable business after exposing the underperformance of your 'realistic' assumptions, then you've got a fair shot of success.

I also don't believe every opinion is equal. Some are more valuable than others. A considered opinion backed by a strong track record in the subject matter is more valuable than just a considered opinion. The difference is in the degree of 'speculating' vs 'knowing'.

To cut through the debate and, importantly, to save time, I ask a few simple questions when I am being pitched anything:

- What do you *know*? How do you know this?
- What do you *think*? Why do you think this?

What I'm doing is finding out the degree of speculation in their argument. Do they 'know' because they have done it before – i.e. their opinion is supported by their track record? Or they have come to their conclusions through logic and reasoning that is the product of their experience? Or have they limited experience in the subject matter but have an opinion they want heard?

Problems can emerge when each of these situations are treated of equal value. It's important to listen to all opinions open-mindedly but the assessment of the value of an individual's opinion needs to be based on both the quality of their reasoning AND the track record that supports it. Treating all opinions equally can lead you away from the truth rather than towards it.

I have seen on many occasions intelligent people, who lack relevant experience, produce logical hypotheses that seem sensible. They diligently research their subject, collect and synthesise data, benchmark against competitors, analyse industry trends and produce charts and reports that seem incontrovertible.

The problem is that that without a track record to support their claims they are speculating. It doesn't mean they are wrong, although they may be, and they might even demonstrate commercial savviness and intuition in coming to their conclusions.

The danger is when their view is accepted as 'truth', rather than what it is – speculation.

Asking the questions listed above can be a great help in this regard especially if the intent is to make the best decisions possible.

What I'm most interested in when analysing any situation is the underlying assumptions of an argument. I prefer, to start with, to get a bullet point list of all the key assumptions before I get anything else. Don't bother me with pages of facts or detailed financial models.

Later on when I'm convinced that the argument is solid, and not based purely on speculation, I'll have a look at this stuff but at the beginning I'm most interested in whether the assumptions seem credible and reasonable.

What I'm also seeking to do is to back-track on the assumptions to assess whether the right (fundamental) questions are being asked – a critical factor for me.

Don't get me wrong I know that less experienced people routinely come up with good (or great) ideas and that is why it is important to retain an open mind when presented with something new. My point is that their credibility and believability needs to be built via a reliable track record of sound reasoning AND achievement in the area in which they are providing their opinion.

Why A Bit of 'Niggle' Is Important

One ingredient that's rarely discussed but vital to any successful and enduring business relationship is a bit of 'niggle'.

(Notice I said 'a bit'.)

I'm not talking about negativity, but rather a degree of healthy tension that should be present when parties with competing (or even aligned) interests come together to do business.

The best business relationships I've had in the past 30 years have involved equal amounts of tummy rubbing and encouragement, exploration, support, brainstorming, vigorous debate and the odd bit of brawling.

The worst relationships have been overweight in tummy rubbing and head nodding, and while wonderfully cheerful achieved very little other than avoiding the underlying issues that brought us together in the first place.

Of course, too much brawling can also produce limited results.

One thing that I do know is that without some *dissent* and *contention* it's difficult to get to the right answer. This is especially important for those infrequent but critical decisions where the stakes are high and the future course is uncertain. With this approach, however, you need to be prepared to encounter and deal with conflict non-defensively and with an open mind and keep the debate constructive.

Many people can't do this. They find it too confronting and instead actively avoid hard, but necessary, discussions.

What they'd prefer is that their team quickly focalises and agrees with their view and the position they are promoting. They're also quick to shut down any discussion if it runs counter to their personal view. What happens as a result is that alternative perspectives and ideas are not put forward and even worse there are no serious attempts to poke holes in the assumptions of the case that is being promoted.

This is the last thing that an organisation needs. What's the point of everyone thinking the same way? What's really valuable is an open-minded willingness to challenge the current thinking, to push out beyond the current boundaries and to encourage diversity of opinion. With these ingredients you'll uncover flaws, bad assumptions and the things that need to change. Without them you stand a good chance of entrenching the problems you are trying to solve and creating more of them in the process.

One guy I know believed so strongly in encouraging dissent among his team that he routinely argued against his own position, picking holes in his own work and encouraging his team to do the same. If they didn't speak up he would ask them questions repeatedly testing their views and searching for a deeper understanding of the matter at hand. He was never happier than when someone found a faulty assumption or bad piece of logic in his own work. His view was simply that it's better to screw up now when the stakes are low rather than later when you've spent money and pushed something 'live' into the market. If it took some argument to get to the truth then, in his view, that was a small price to pay.

What I know is that dissent, conflict, argument, niggle or whatever you choose to call it is a critical ingredient to making the best possible decisions. Consensus, when it finally comes, should be as a result of the constructive debate that preceded it. To get there however you may need to speak up, argue, rock the boat and take a contrarian view.

This kind of debate often creates a bit of 'niggle' because it's not always what you want to hear. It might grate at you and make you angry. It might make you defensive, and you start using dangerous expressions such as "They just don't get it!" when the truth may be quite different.

It might seem easier to just ignore it. But if the person giving the advice is reputable and their motives are genuine, they're probably worth listening to.

For me, 'niggle' is the secret sauce of successful and enduring business relationships. It challenges the status quo, which is always a good thing. It means those protecting the 'old' have to clash with those promoting the 'new'. And, if for no other reason, that's why a bit of 'niggle' is important.

Keep Asking Those Dumb Questions

Dumb questions are rarely dumb. The best people I know understand this, and ask lots of questions no matter how simple, naïve or dumb they may sound. They'd rather be ridiculed than make decisions armed with less than a clear understanding of all relevant information.

The collapse of the once all-conquering Enron is a dramatic example. Before its bankruptcy in late 2001 Enron was one of the world's largest conglomerates, with 22,000 staff and reported revenues of US$101b. Fortune Magazine named it America's Most Innovative Company for six years straight. It was untouchable, or so everyone thought.

It started to unravel when a reporter, Bethany McLean, innocently asked Enron CEO Jeff Skilling a 'dumb' question: "How does Enron make money?" Skilling abused the reporter, calling her ill-prepared and incompetent.

But she was the first person who'd ever asked whether Enron was actually profitable.

Soon afterwards Skilling verbally attacked a Wall Street Analyst who'd asked for Enron's quarterly balance sheet with the earnings statement for the third time. The analyst pointed out to Skilling that Enron was the only publicly listed company that couldn't release a balance sheet simultaneously with its earnings statements. Nobody else had raised it, so Skilling replied with, "Well, thank you very much, we appreciate that... asshole".

Inevitably it was discovered that Enron had *never* made any money, and Skilling is now in jail serving 14 years for multiple counts of fraud and insider trading.

A similar thing happened with the U.S. mortgage market collapse in 2007. Homebuyers often didn't understand how interest rate resets affected their mortgages, taking on debt they inevitably couldn't repay. Banks ignored the risks and encouraged them to borrow more while paying mortgage brokers high commissions to write more business.

At the same time, regulators praised complex and risky mortgaged-backed securities. And many financial commentators and economists still insisted the financial markets were in good shape. Few understood what was really going on, but everyone acted as if they did.

Mark Twain once said, "Whenever you find yourself on the side of the majority, it's time to pause and reflect".

Would things have been any different if someone had asked the dumb, obvious questions?

It's hard to tell. While it may not have stopped the problems, it may have contained the damage. Part of the problem seemed to be that people didn't want to look dumb, and so just went along with the consensus view. They didn't understand what was happening, or why. And I'm guessing that greed played a (major) part too.

The best solution is to ask questions about anything you don't understand. There's little point in staying quiet and trying to appear smart when you can ask obvious questions that could improve your understanding and lead to better decisions.

Here are a few 'dumb' questions I've found particularly useful over the years:

- I'm not sure I understand. Is [this] what you're saying?
- Can you explain it in another way that's easier for me to understand?
- Can you simply explain to me why we're doing this?
- What if we didn't do this/did something else?
- How do you know what you're saying is correct?

It takes guts to ask the dumb questions. You have to put the fear of looking stupid below the goal of making the best possible decisions.

But the payoff is worth it.

I've come to realise that a curious mind and a healthy willingness to publicly say "I don't understand" can be just as important to a prosperous future as anything else you do.

How I Like To Invest

As a young banker I watched Warwick Fairfax, armed with a recently acquired Harvard MBA and $1.7b of bank funding, privatise the venerable media company Fairfax Media. Not a bad effort for a 26-year-old.

Unfortunately the high gearing and 20% interest rates proved too much, and the company was placed into receivership three years later.

This was a typical 1980s style leveraged buyout—too much debt, a half-baked plan, and plenty of 'advisors' around the table getting paid big fees to make it happen.

It never really had a chance.

Since then I've invested directly in several businesses. Some were strong performers, others weren't. Reflecting on those successes and failures, three ingredients (what I call the three Ps) need to be present for a business to be an attractive investment proposition for me.

- **People**. There needs to be a good team in place and an exceptional leader. People I can trust and count on. People with a plan for the future and the capability to execute it. Determined people who treat company money like their own, and make hard decisions when they need to. Doers, not talkers.
- **Product**. The product must solve a genuine market problem at a fair price. The business must have a strong niche that's growing, and a point of difference that protects it from its competition. And I need to be able to understand this quickly.

   I'm not interested in businesses with high, unsustainable margins, or those selling cheap commodity-type products. They're just too vulnerable. And it's the same with companies operating in sectors where very large, well-run innovative companies are entrenched.

- **Place.** I invest close to home where I understand the local culture and how business is done. I don't invest offshore, and even interstate can be a stretch for me. I stay close to my own backyard because it's where my strongest networks are and where I understand things best. Distance adds complexity, and staying close to home helps me solve problems quickly and keeps me productive.

While a business that ticks all three P's is ideal, those that tick two out of the three may also be acceptable in certain circumstances. But one P is never enough for me to do a deal, and whatever happens the people equation *must* be right.

I'm patient and always invest slowly. I'd rather miss an opportunity than invest in a bad one. I also never invest more than I can comfortably lose (i.e. if I lost the lot it would just make me limp for a while rather than being a death blow).

Finally, I never invest in highly leveraged deals. Young Warwick Fairfax taught me that lesson.

Sometimes I've made money, and sometimes I've lost the lot. When I lost money it was always because I ignored the three P's in my eagerness to get a deal done.

Every. Single. Time.

And whenever I made money, those three P's were all ticked.

It all comes down to the fundamentals: good people, a good proposition and plan, and a growing market. It seems like a simple formula, but from my experience it's notoriously difficult to implement well.

Trust Your Gut Instinct

For any decision, even when you do all the predictive research and future scenario testing, you will never be able to fully close the 'risk gap' covering all the endless possibilities of what might happen in the future. The future is unpredictable and being in possession of all the information required to *fully* mitigate *all* risks is unrealistic.

This doesn't mean you shouldn't research deeply; just don't expect that the data and insights you collect will provide *all* the answers you are seeking.

The same applies to listening to the advice of well-meaning friends, families and advisors.

What this means is that at some point you will need to take a leap of faith into the unknown and rely on your own intuition and common sense to make the best decisions you can.

When I started Calendar Club back in 1995 I shared my business plan with my friends and family to get some external validation. Most of them advised me against proceeding.

A good mate of mine, who is now a successful businessman in his own right, told me bluntly: "Forget about it mate. It'll never work".

Other people were more diplomatic, but their advice was the same: don't do it.

Today that business is the market leader in its sector, and continues to grow every year. It has a great brand that's recognised widely by consumers across Australia and New Zealand.

In short, it was (and still is) a winner.

All the advice people gave me early on was well-intentioned, and none of it was mean-spirited. In their minds they were looking after my best interests. I listened to their counsel, but made my own decisions. I'd done the research and analysis (they hadn't) and I knew that while there was risk involved, success was possible with hard work and some luck. I pushed the button, moved forward and never looked back.

GK Chesterton once wrote, "I owe my success to having listened respectfully to the very best advice, and then going away and doing the exact opposite". He makes a good point: listen to your own instincts and trust your gut when making key decisions. Sometimes you'll need to take calculated risks, but that's different to being rash or making ill-informed decisions.

I made the worst business decisions when I put more faith in the advice of others (including so-called experts) than my gut instincts. When I trust my gut I usually do well, and when I ignore it I usually do badly.

I don't make snap decisions, but I don't delay unnecessarily either. I get outside advice when I need it, and collect information from wherever I can. To make an educated choice I need to know enough, not everything. And when I feel uncomfortable I don't proceed. (Admittedly, I became better at this as the years went by.)

The trick in trusting your gut is to block out all the noise and distractions around you. Focus on the essence of the matter at hand, and pull it apart until you understand it at its core. Most issues are less complicated than they first appear, and doing this really simplifies the decision-making process.

Trusting your gut is an important business skill. You get better at it with experience. Kenny Rogers' famous line, "You got to know when to hold 'em, know when to fold 'em, know when to walk away, know when to run" sums it up nicely.

Culture Counts

In theory, running a business should be easy. You and your team create a product or service. Your customers give you money for it. You use that money to create more/better products or services. Invent, reinvent, repeat.

Unfortunately, we're not robots. We're human. And that brings a whole bunch of emotions and feelings into play. Which is why having a good culture in your organisation isn't just desirable.

It's vital.

An Organisation's Core Values Are More Than Just Words On A Page

When companies start talking about their core values I switch off. It usually means they're trying to sell me something, or convince me they're better than they really are. And it's the same when they publish them on their website or in their marketing material.

In my experience, if you're compelled to describe your core values in a sales pitch then they're probably not true.

The trouble is these core values statements are often created on a weekend retreat or during a two-hour workshop. They then get hashed around by a couple of senior managers and approved by the CEO. Somebody types them up, puts them on the website, and frames a copy for the reception area.

And they're never referred to again.

The problem is they reflect the rosy view of two or three people at the top, rather than the realistic view of the masses. They describe what the company *wants* to be, not what it *is*.

If companies were honest, they'd admit their *true* core values (which they demonstrate by their behaviour) may be vastly different from what they purport them to be. It's human nature to over-state your core values, and very common to make them aspirational. But unless they're true they don't mean much.

Core values embody the collective behaviours of everyone in the organisation. They're rooted in the day-to-day reality of how you do business, and how you deal with (and treat) your partners, customers, suppliers and staff.

I base my business interests on three core values. They haven't changed in twenty years:

1. We must keep innovating, even when there's no pressing need to.
2. If we say we'll do it, we do it.
3. We must be kind.

I'm not perfect by any means, and I screw things up regularly. But these core values help me stay on track, and force me to regulate my behaviour when I need to.

Continuing to relentlessly innovate is a core requirement of any business, in my view. Similarly 'if we say we'll do it, we do it' covers off on the need to be honest, reliable and act with integrity.

Of all the values on the list, being kind is the least understood. It's not the same as niceness, which rarely costs anything. Kindness is about helping, even when there's nothing in it for you. It's about helping when it's painful, and it would be easier to just ignore the situation and leave it for someone else to fix.

It also costs you something every time you give it.

Kindness can manifest itself in many ways. I can recall a few occasions when, after exhausting all other options, I had to be brutally frank to force much-needed change and make people see sense. It isn't always appreciated, and it certainly isn't enjoyable. It may even hurt a relationship for a while.

It would be easier for me to just go along with the head-nodders and ignore the issues. And sometimes I wish I could do that. But I know I can't if I want to live my values daily.

If your motives are pure, and your behaviour is consistent, people will eventually (and sometimes grudgingly) concede that your actions were underpinned by kindness.

Take another look at your core values statement, and compare them to the actual behaviours of your organisation. Are they in line, or are they different?

If they accurately reflect the collective behaviours of your organisation, take a bow. But if they don't, then they're nothing more than words on a page.

Which means you've got some work to do.

Friendly And Intense

Right from the time I opened the doors of my first business, Calendar Club, I had a goal to create a motivating and inspiring place to work. I had worked in several companies, observed others and read about many more. I wanted my business to be the best of the best. A friendly place. A place with a can-do attitude where people believed anything was possible. A place where the team felt motivated to take up the fight that every start-up must take up. To push hard. To be mavericks.

And ultimately to upset the 'apple-cart' of the sector in which we operated.

We succeeded in large part due to our culture. Money was tight and we had to make our resources stretch to incredible lengths as we scaled up. If there was not a general willingness to step up among the team we would not have made it.

The camaraderie, team work and willingness to go the extra mile under extreme pressure (at times) meant we achieved a lot *without a* lot. Critically we always behaved as underdogs. These behaviours were the *intangibles* that propelled us to market leadership in a relatively short period of time.

If I had to describe the culture of that business I'd probably borrow words from Jeff Bezos, founder of Amazon, when he described his own company's culture like this: "Our culture is friendly and intense, but if push comes to shove we'll settle for intense".

I like that, because it represents the reality of business. And it describes Calendar Club's culture perfectly.

'Intense' is important. Intense means you're focused on achieving results and pushing a business forward. It means that you are willing to hunt down the *truth* about any matter even if it leads to difficult discussions. It also recognises that the status quo is a dangerous place and needs to be routinely challenged.

This can be uncomfortable at times. And that's why being friendly is important but only as long as it doesn't interfere with making the *very* best decisions.

What I drummed into the Calendar Club team, and every team I have been involved with since, was that we all get paid to do more than to just manage the steady state and the status quo. We *really* get paid to innovate, to get that next breakthrough and we can't do that without intensity in our culture—friendly or otherwise.

But It Should Be Fun Too.

It may be intense but it should be fun too.

Shouldn't it?

What if people loved coming to work because it was so much fun? Would productivity increase? Would the culture improve?

Yes...

Then why aren't more workplaces fun to work at?

Beats me...

How about your workplace – how does it rate in the fun stakes?

- Are people, including the 'chiefs', regularly seen laughing, joking and smiling?
- Do you stop and celebrate the funny things that happen?
- Do you have regular fun/team-building activities organised?

How did you score?

If not well, then do something about it. Past a big goofy smile on your face. Share a joke. Tell a funny story. Make someone laugh. Offer a gentle word of encouragement. Organise a fun activity*.

Start small.

A smile, a joke and a quiet word from the boss can go a long way to improving morale and increasing productivity. Never forget that people respond to being noticed, included and appreciated.

At a deeper level, fun and laughter creates bonds and friendships and removes barriers, hierarchical and cultural, leading to more creativity and productivity.

The economic pay-off to creating a fun and happy work environment can be more loyal and productive employees. Absenteeism and tardiness will decrease as people actually look forward to going to work. Taken to the next level, staff turnover will fall as the happiness quotient increases.

Fun and work go well together, or at least they should. Work doesn't have to be boring or unenjoyable. A fun work environment reduces stress, anxiety and boredom. If people are in good spirits then they will be calmer and better able to tolerate and cope with anything that comes up. None of which is bad for business.

'Fun' activities do not need to be expensive and when you cost them versus the benefits achieved they will be very cheap. Whatever you do, make sure it is the employees not the managers who come up with the activities. This approach will be received much better by everyone.

The Effects Of Negative Talk

Everywhere I go I hear businesses complaining about how tough their sector is. Many of them blame external factors for their problems. Government policy. Exchange rates. Low consumer confidence. Greedy landlords. Pressure from online or offshore competitors.

The dog ate my homework, maybe?

The problem with negative talk is it becomes a self-fulfilling prophecy. Talking it down and generally being negative will eventually become reality. It will rub off on your staff, who will then lower their performance expectations and blame the market too. Eventually they'll switch off, believing nothing they do will make a difference. Declining sales and profits will become accepted because 'it's not our fault'.

And when it reaches *that* point, it's time to go and find something else to do.

I'm not saying you shouldn't be realistic. Just don't be negative. And there's a big difference between the two.

Negative is easy. Saying "It's not my fault" or "The market's crap" or "We're doing no worse than anyone else" is just a cop out. Sure it's easy and convenient to blame someone or something else, but it doesn't overcome the challenges you're facing *or* help you get better.

Setting the right example through language and behaviour is a key requirement for all business leaders. You want your people to feel motivated about making a difference. Right?

It's even more important when times get tough. Leaders need to show confidence during these difficult times, and work hard to inspire their people and assure them everything will be okay.

So don't throw your hands in the air and complain how tough trading conditions are. Or play the blame game. Instead, knuckle down, get tough, be positive, solve problems and move forward. And keep doing it day after day.

Because that's what we're paid to do. Not to make excuses.

Ditch The Corporate Speak

"We need to do some out-of-the-box thinking from the get-go with sufficient granularity in the drill-down phase to ensure our value-added strategy is consistent with our core values and beliefs."

This statement was actually made by the CEO of a $400m company to his senior management team. Nobody questioned what the statement actually meant, and many of them just nodded their heads in agreement.

Huh?

This is just nonsense language that means nothing, and I'm not sure why companies do it. Maybe they're not even aware they *are* doing it, or genuinely believe it creates unity, energy, vitality and a team culture.

It doesn't.

All it does is rob the company of its individual voices, stifle the flow of ideas, weaken customer relationships and demotivate staff. It turns the individual voices of many into the single voice of an anonymous corporate identity.

And that's bad, especially when consumers want closer, more personalised connections with the companies they deal with.

What companies *should* be doing is creating distinct personalities with different perspectives within their organisations to breathe life into them. But you can't do that if you talk like a robot or punctuate every sentence with corporate speak.

Use plain English, and speak in the language of your customers and the wider community. You're no cleverer than they are, so don't behave as if you are.

A great culture is built on two fundamentals: credible, engaged management, and employees with fire in their eyes. Not a bunch of silly words that mean nothing.

Executive Perks Are Bad For Business

This scenario occurs all too often. A group of employees are booked to attend a meeting interstate or overseas. They arrive at the airport and saunter over to the economy-class check-in line, which as always is long and crowded. There's excitement among the group about the travel plans and the good times ahead.

Then one of the group notices the boss over at the business class check-in counter nonchalantly joking with the check-in staff. The boss never mentioned he was flying business class and everyone else was flying economy. They make a few uncomplimentary comments about the different rules for different people, and their excitement starts to drain.

This situation can manifest itself in many different ways— private executive bathrooms, luxury car allowances, and different hotel standards for different pay grades.

If you want to build an inclusive, engaged workforce, then these perks should be outlawed.

It's all nonsense and fluff anyway. If you can't bear to fly economy then no-one else should either. It may cost your business some money, but it will resonate strongly with your employees and they'll love you for it. And if you can't afford it then *everyone* should fly economy, including you. They'll respect you for that too.

The same applies to reserved parking spaces at the office. They make no sense at all. Whoever shows up first should get the pick of the car park. Why penalise the early birds by making them walk past empty executive car spaces on their way to their desk? If you're that important, show up first and claim whatever space you like.

Family businesses are particularly bad at this, and my advice to them is simple. The business isn't about the family. It's about the business. So do whatever's in the best interests of the business.

Employees love the idea of having one set of rules for everyone. It breaks down the hierarchy, and helps to build a great culture. That should be reason enough to do it. The only thing that stands in the way is management giving up a few soft perks that don't mean anything.

It seems like a simple choice to me.

How To Rid Yourself Of Company Politics

Company politics exist for one reason: to advance careers or agendas by means other than merit or contribution. People either get rewarded when they don't deserve it, or don't get rewarded when they *do* deserve it.

Interestingly, sometimes it's the least political CEOs who run the most political organisations—often without even knowing it. Perhaps they're out of their depth or play favourites. Inevitably it means they don't base rewards solely on merit. They hand out pay rises, promotions or other benefits to make people happy, or to keep louder, more political staff members quiet.

They react to staff 'noise' instead of closely reviewing performance and the results it produced.

While this might seem to work, at least in the short term, what it actually does is alienate the less political staff who may in fact be stronger contributors.

Unfortunately it's impossible to *subjectively* treat everyone the same, no matter how hard you try. Environments like these are fertile ground for corporate politics to take hold and flourish.

The only effective way to manage people is to base career advancement purely on merit and contribution, and not on any other factor. Creating a win-win situation is key. Advancement should be based on achieving objective, measurable outcomes that create value for the organisation, and career and financial opportunities for the staff. If your staff achieve the agreed outcomes, they should be rewarded. If they don't, then they shouldn't be.

And the decision should be black and white and totally unambiguous.

Make this clear in your organisation (through position descriptions, *objective* performance agreements, incentive structures, career development plans and a disciplined review process) and you'll wipe out a lot of the politics that exists in your organisation.

Yes, it will take time and effort to put it in place, and discipline to maintain it. But what other choice do you really have?

(You may think this sounds naïve, but think about it. Why else does politics exist in an organisation? Most people don't actually know. They just blame others and accept it as being a

permanent feature of organisations. But it doesn't need to be, especially if you understand the real causes of it.)

Culture and Brand –Two Peas In A Pod

There's more to a brand than just the logo on top of your letterhead. It's not something your customers see. It's what they feel. It can't be touched or smelt, but you know what it is.

To describe it another way, brand is interchangeable with reputation. And it directly reflects the internal culture of an organisation. It's a *fulfilled* promise to a marketplace that resonates with it to the point where the marketplace values it.

At least that's what a *good* brand is. Bad brands are the complete opposite.

A brand is developed the moment an organisation is founded, and is the living breathing embodiment of the organisation's cumulative and collective behaviours from that point on.

Brand acts like a two-way lens between the company and its marketplace. It's a dynamic process where a company's behaviour is constantly reviewed and assessed by its customers and users. These continual interactions act like a perpetual, unrelenting scorecard quietly and seamlessly ticking away.

Every single interaction has a positive or negative influence on a brand. Every single user has a say in how it's perceived. They vote by deciding whether they'll spend money with a company, or even come back. They vote with their opinion and how they talk about the brand. It's the result of these votes that ultimately determines a company's reputation, and whether or not its brand will endure.

But do you know what your brand reputation really is?

My advice to you is, don't ask your management team. They might be drinking the Kool-Aid and have a distorted opinion. Their view may be aspirational, not grounded in reality. They might even be ignoring some inconvenient truths too uncomfortable to acknowledge. Or revert to what was 'agreed' at the annual management retreat when everyone sat around deciding what the brand is or should be.

Whatever the case, chances are what the company thinks about the brand is different to what the market thinks, at least in some ways. And therein lies the great disconnect of business.

If you really want to understand what the market thinks about your brand, do a Google search. And then check the conversations on Facebook, blogs, forums and other social media platforms. It's the fastest way to get a read on what the market really thinks of your brand.

But that's not enough. What you read online may only be the views of the noisy minority. So you have to dig deeper. Head to the streets and talk to your suppliers, customers, ex-customers and front line field staff. Ask *them* how you shape up. They'll probably have a much better idea of your brand reality than anyone sitting in a cubicle at HQ.

They key is to understand what *you* think compared to what the *market* thinks. If there's a gap, close it quickly. The gap is where most problems occur.

Why? Because when expectations aren't aligned, conflict and disappointment is inevitable. But when expectations are closely aligned there's little potential for conflict or disappointment, which helps the business endure and keeps it profitable.

It's sometimes the little things that hurt a brand badly. Things that are easy to fix but are missed or ignored because the focus is elsewhere. However, if they are left unattended, they can cause serious damage.

Airlines are a great case study in this respect. They deal with hundreds of thousands, if not millions, of passengers every year. Most of the time they provide a seamless service that's simple, easy to use and meets their customers' expectations. But when something goes wrong it can be a calamity that damages their brand quickly—and possibly permanently.

Here's my personal story about why I no longer travel with a discount Australian airline.

It began with a rapid-fire one-and-a-half day interstate business trip. By the time I got to the airport for my return flight I was tired. The flight was delayed. Okay, no problem.

It finally took off at about 7.30pm. At 8.30pm it was in a holding pattern over Melbourne. At 9.00pm we were advised that Melbourne airport was closed due to bad weather and the flight was returning to Sydney.

The 200 passengers on board instantly became annoyed and frustrated. But it wasn't the airline's fault. You can't land if the airport is closed.

When we got back to Sydney we were escorted into a departure lounge and told we were now booked on a 9.30 am flight the following morning.

And that's *all* we were told.

When a passenger asked about overnight accommodation, the reply was blunt: It's not the airline's fault (which it wasn't) so you'll have to sort yourselves out. At this stage it was after 10pm, and despite the collective groan they didn't offer any other assistance.

It was a massive personal inconvenience for me. My plans for the next morning were shot—two meetings had to be rescheduled, and I missed the school tour of my oldest son's school. I was also more than $400 out of pocket, including the over-priced $330 hotel room I found only after a dozen phone calls to other hotels that were already booked out.

And without a fresh change of clothes I had to re-wear what I'd worn the previous day.

But at least I could get a room. One passenger said he couldn't afford a hotel room, and would probably rent a car and park in a nearby street overnight. Or, failing that, sleep on a park bench.

Next day, I was in line at the airport 90 minutes before my flight's departure time. After 20 minutes I was almost at the front of the queue.

Suddenly I was told I had to wait as 30 or so earlier departing passengers were called forward. Why was I being asked to wait when I was doing the airline a favour by arriving much earlier than I needed to be? And why do the 'late' customers get priority?

I waited in line, silently fuming. It was a minor inconvenience compared to what had already happened, but it still added to my frustration.

When I finally got to the front of the line there was no acknowledgement of what had happened in the previous 12 hours. I was simply directed to a robotic check-in clerk devoid of personality and warmth. I headed to the departure gate, only to find my flight had been delayed for an hour. Another impersonal announcement from someone hiding behind the service desk: "Due to a late departure from Melbourne, blah, blah, blah".

Frustration overload.

This company let down their customers at every touch point. It would have cost them nothing to be nice, or to genuinely apologise. To make a fuss about the people who'd been so grossly inconvenienced. To *not* make the same passengers wait (again) at check-in—especially if they'd arrived early. To leave the service desk, circulate through the departure lounge and speak directly to customers with a smile and a word of encouragement. To have someone more senior than a flight attendant greet them at check-in and speak to them. To offer the stranded passengers a coffee voucher. (Even a free drink on the flight home would have been something.) To find out room availability and prices of nearby hotels while the plane was heading back to Sydney to help stranded passengers find a hotel once they were on the ground.

Or for the CEO to send a subsequent email to the affected passengers to apologise for the inconvenience and thank them for their patience and understanding.

Instead they just threw up their hands claiming it wasn't their fault (which was true), did the bare minimum by arranging a replacement flight the next day, and then went about their business as if nothing had happened. But in doing so they demonstrated their shallow understanding of cause and effect, and the real underlying personality of their company.

Organisations with high emotional intelligence understand it's not about blame or fault, statistics or ratings. It's about being able to walk in their customers' shoes and understand their frustration and pain. It's about realising people are individuals, and that they're all different. It's about reacting to uncomfortable events quickly and effectively.

Ultimately, it's about showing you *really* care.

It makes me wonder when the airline's senior executives last staffed the check-in counter. Shepherded people through the check-in line. Spoke to passengers in the departure lounge. Walked the aisle in-flight serving coffee.

Or stood in the front line when a flight was cancelled or significantly delayed.

The airline didn't do anything majorly wrong. They may even consider organising another plane at relatively short notice a triumph. But they failed because they didn't care enough about their customers' inconvenience, and treated them like numbers instead of people.

In the end they exposed their 'brand' AND culture for all their customers to see. And it wasn't a pretty sight.

Leading by Example

There's a saying that goes something like, "Managers make people follow them. Leaders make people want to follow them". And I think it sums up leadership pretty well. You can't force it on people. It needs to be earned by doing the right thing (which isn't always the nice thing), and giving everyone a chance to have their say.

And a chance to shine.

Becoming A Great Leader

What makes a great leader? I've listened to dozens of people try to answer this seemingly simple question. And it was years before I heard an answer that gave me that "Aha!" moment.

It finally came from an odd source: an insight from the ancient philosopher Lao Tzu who said:

"Go to the people. Learn from them. Honour them. Start with what they know. Build on what they have. But of a great leader who talks little, when the work is done and his aim is fulfilled, the people will say 'We did this ourselves'."

Tzu talks of the people—the team—and how the leader's primary role is to mould them so they can reach their full potential. It's hard, unrelenting and selfless work, with little kudos attached to it. And at its centre is two-way respect—something not easily or quickly acquired.

What *isn't* important is winning awards, media exposure or any other type of personal glory.

Tzu's words are a wake-up call to modern-day leadership. They highlight the timeless values of selflessness, mutual respect, and the need to be driven and focused. Taking it further, you need to care deeply about your people, and constantly look for ways to develop them and ultimately improve their lives. Do that, and they'll repay you by the bucket load. But if you don't, there's a good chance you'll end up with a dysfunctional, unmotivated workforce.

If you're looking for a real leader, don't expect to find them in the obvious places (e.g. on centre stage with microphone in hand, expounding the latest triumph). Instead, go to the back of the room. They're probably having a quiet drink and smiling at their people who are saying, "We did this ourselves".

The Universal Job Description Of Leaders

The best job description for a leader I ever heard came during a training workshop I conducted for a corporate business. It came from one of the team's new senior members, and she nailed it in just 29 words.

"My job description as a leader is to work on the big stuff and the small stuff and leave everything else to middle managers and staff to sort out."

It was a simple but brilliant answer that cut to the heart of leadership.

The big stuff obviously involves spending time in deep reflection to discover a purpose, create a vision, choose a strategic direction and set out the key objectives. It's future-focused, an essential part of the job, and can turn a business from a rambling, unfocused, pointless mess into a juggernaut.

A key part of the big stuff is selling the vision and strategy to your team. If they buy in to it, you're on your way. To do that, you need to set a strong personal example, demonstrate the possibilities, and reassure your team and give them hope for a prosperous future. Your job is as much to inspire as to confront realities pragmatically. You have to make people comfortable with what the company is doing and where it's heading.

The small stuff is important too, but a lot of leaders neglect it. It's those niggling, seemingly insignificant matters that seem to keep coming up and taking company resources to fix. They might be process matters, relationship matters or a myriad of other things. But they all share one common characteristic: they slow progress down.

They might seem small, but some invariably point to much larger 'iceberg' issues lurking below the surface that, if left unchecked, could be potentially disastrous later on.

An important part of leadership is to always be on the lookout for these points of vulnerability. The warning signs may be vague or small, but that doesn't mean they're not important. Dealing with them quickly is critical. It's the essence of focusing on the small stuff.

It reminds me of the TV show, Undercover Boss. In one episode a female garbage truck driver was forced to pee into a can instead of visiting a toilet because her pick-up quotas were so tough that even a few minutes for a toilet break would mean she wouldn't hit her allocated daily targets.

The Uncover Boss had no idea that this was happening.

But why not?

The answer is obvious (and cautionary).

The boss' decision to increase quotas was made away from the coal-face, using faulty information or the opinions of his colleagues who were obviously no better informed than he was.

What's wrong with instructing one of your managers to spend a day or two in a truck testing the likely effects of the quota change before the decision was made?

Part of the problem may be that as executives move up the ladder they choose to distance themselves from what is happening on the ground. They delegate this to somebody else to worry about and stay detached from what is happening at the grass roots of their business. They rely on second-hand, filtered information provided by colleagues and end up with a sanitised view of reality.

When it comes to leading businesses I've learnt you can't sit in an ivory tower, removed from the practical day-to-day realities of your businesses. But you can't get bogged down in the endless grind of daily minutia either. Getting the balance right is pretty much the job description of a leader.

And ultimately their greatest challenge.

The Smartest Person In The Room

One of the silliest situations I have ever observed was the behaviour of a new CEO in a business meeting a few months into his role. At the start of the meeting he announced to everyone in earshot that, "One of the things I assume whenever I attend a meeting or gathering is that I'm the smartest guy in the room. Consequently I make most of the decisions myself".

Yikes!

It was a dumb move. In the space of a few seconds he downgraded the collective intelligence of his entire team. Worse still, he did it publicly. It showed no respect, and immediately deflated his team. They retreated into their shells, became disgruntled, and over time lost their care factor. A great culture, carefully crafted over many years, began to slowly unravel because of the stupidity of an egotistical fool claiming to be the smartest person in the room.

It's bad enough to think you are the smartest person in the room let alone announce it out loud. It serves no purpose at all and is incredibly self-indulgent and downright dangerous. It's also (highly) unlikely to be true.

As you move up the ladder in business your specific *technical* skills become less important than your ability to manage people and more precisely teams of people. A great engineer, marketer, accountant or even entrepreneur will be ineffectual as a business leader unless they can get people to follow them. This only occurs if the leader's behaviour is predictable and consistent (in a good way, of course).

In my own experience, the best leaders I know have very predictable behaviour. They are demanding too and expect a lot of their people. They want to discover, access and develop the very best parts of their people's talents. They stretch them but are careful not to break them and they do this in a *safe* environment where everyone is encouraged to excel.

Working with leaders like this isn't always comfortable, and can be quite confronting. Inevitably some people won't cope and will move on. But for those who stay, the payoff is an exhilarating ride and a richly satisfying experience of self-discovery and achievement.

In the end, a leader's effectiveness is determined by their ability to influence others to believe in them and their mission. It's not about being the smartest person in the room. It's not even about being the leader. It's about the quality and productivity of their team, and their ability to unlock and capitalise on its potential.

That is the essential goal of leadership, and the only thing that really matters.

Healthy Paranoia

Intel founder Andy Groves once said the mantra he used to run his company was that "only the paranoid survive". Groves understood that what worked yesterday might not work tomorrow, and that a company's beliefs, practices and behaviours needed to be challenged regularly. This type of paranoia becomes a relentless desire to find new and better ways to attack old problems and exploit new opportunities.

To do that you can't hang your hat on past successes, continuously talk about last year's results or pine for the good old days. And you can't protect your business' sacred cows or tolerate behaviour that holds it back.

That's why you rarely find successful leaders suffering from delusions of grandeur, complacency or hubris. They challenge everything in their quest to find the best solutions possible to push their businesses forward. And they focus on one thing—the ability to execute their future plan.

Most leaders' paranoia comes from external events. Will new products, competitors, economic or regulatory threats emerge that could de-rail our business? Will customers continue to pay a fair price for our products? Where are the vulnerabilities that competitors could exploit, or could stop customers buying from us?

These are the issues that keep leaders awake at night. They don't switch off. It grows into a heightened sense of urgency, even impatience, to get things done quickly. Time is their worst enemy, and they know they need to use every minute wisely.

I learnt these lessons first-hand. I didn't have a choice—it was learn or perish. Even after all these years I still have a healthy degree of paranoia and find it hard to switch off. I'm always working the angles to uncover vulnerabilities and opportunities in every business I'm associated with.

I carry a notebook wherever I go to record thoughts, ideas and other random observations. It's led to several opportunities I would have otherwise missed. It helps that I love what I do, and that I wouldn't have it any other way.

Paranoia might seem an odd trait for a leader. But you'll find the great ones have it in spades.

What's Wrong with Being a Benevolent Dictator?

It would be nice if businesses operated as a democracy, with every team member having an equal vote. Unfortunately you'd end up attending endless meetings and drinking copious amounts of coffee while trying to satisfy everyone's pet projects and minor grievances. It's just not possible, and would waste too much valuable company time.

That being said, everyone in an organisation should have a voice. And it's the leaders' job to make sure they're heard, and their views are considered and evaluated.

But while they should all have an equal say (and be allowed to get involved in the decision-making process) they shouldn't all get an equal vote in the final decision. In the end someone has to make the final call, and it should be one person who's considered everyone's view—*not* a committee.

In most cases, a good model for business is a benevolent dictatorship. 'Benevolence' means being pre-disposed to acts of goodness. And a 'dictator' is someone who has absolute power.

The word 'dictator' has a negative connotation these days, thanks to power-hungry lunatics such as Hitler, Saddam and Gadhafi. But these dictators weren't benevolent or respected, and their actions were based purely on self-interest.

Benevolent dictators, on the other hand, do the right thing. They know that leadership is not a popularity contest and, with that knowledge, grudgingly accept the responsibilities that ultimate authority demands and put their own interests behind the needs of the wider organisation. They also show a readiness to act decisively, even in desperate situations, knowing the buck stops with them.

This only works if the leader has built respect with their team (something that takes time to achieve), and is the natural consequence of demonstrating personal capability and commitment. So be ethical, kind, transparent and inclusive, but also decisive. And make sure you focus on building a strong team to support you.

If that sums up a benevolent dictator, is there really anything wrong with it?

Don't Be A Saviour.

There's always a temptation to jump in and re-write inadequate reports and take over projects from team-mates when they're floundering. It feels like the right thing to do, for both the person involved and for the organisation itself. Get the job done. Help out. Be the saviour. That's what 'team players' are supposed to do, right?

I used to think that, but not anymore. What it actually does is slow down progress in the long run rather than speed it up. By repeatedly stepping in to save the day you're stifling your team's development and making them more reliant on you instead of less.

And that's not good.

These days I hand back sub-standard work with some suggestions and ask for it to be done again. And while I make it clear I'm available to help, I won't do the work for them. If it takes them a few times to get it right that's fine by me. I don't subscribe to the theory that "It will only take me five minutes to fix so I may as well do it myself". You need to give people the freedom to screw up. Failure is an efficient teacher, and if you catch people before they hit the ground they won't develop as fast as they otherwise might. Yes it's painful, and takes longer at the start, but it's a much quicker way to learn and better for everyone in the long run.

What can also help is asking, "First tell me what you know, then tell me what you think". It can quickly establish how much they know about a particular issue so you can more accurately target how you'll help them. Setting realistic expectations also helps.

Being a 'saviour' might inflate your ego, but it's a short-term fix that will impede your organisation's long-term development. No business can run effectively if critical tasks can only be performed by a small number of people. What happens when they're away? Or busy? Nothing.

And that's not good for anyone.

The Board and the CEO

And now a word about the Board and the CEO.

To be the CEO of a medium to large business you need a big ego. Successful businesses aren't built by shrinking violets, or by humble men or women. A CEO needs a strong backbone and an uncommon strength of character. They're driven, are prepared to take risks, and fight like alley cats when cornered. They like being in charge, and in a lot of cases define themselves by their role. They're not afraid to challenge the existing order. They work hard, are time-poor, and make a lot of personal sacrifices to achieve their business objectives.

To be successful a CEO needs a lot of help. A good management team, excellent advisors and some great staff are all prerequisites. Some outside capital may also be needed, and if that's the case then a board of directors will probably be needed too.

Let's talk about the board for a moment. The board has four main functions:

- to hire the CEO
- to approve and monitor the company's strategic plan and progress
- to keep shareholders informed of company performance
- to deal with compliance and governance matters.

The CEO and the management team are responsible for running the company.

A good board can be of enormous benefit to a business. But a bad board can be disastrous. The key is to align expectations to a common set of outcomes. If all efforts point in the same direction and the same performance standards are universally applied, it can remove a lot of problems and tensions.

Unfortunately it's never that easy.

In recent times two trends have caused problems for boards and the businesses they represent. One problem is the focus on short-term results. The public market's obsession with six-monthly financial results has to some degree influenced the actions companies take. Boards can spend a lot of time trying to manage the opportunities and fallout from constantly moving share prices, rather than longer-term strategic matters.

Performance decline over several successive periods can sometimes result in drastic action being taken, which can have severe long-term consequences for a business. The desire to quickly return the business to previously enjoyed levels of profitability could in fact be the worst thing to do if it fundamentally damages the business.

What's important during these times is to make sure there's balance between the short-term pressures and the long-term objectives. A business without a clear long-term vision will default to short-term initiatives and lurch from one "next big thing" (or crisis) to the next. The role of the board is to make sure this balance is understood, and that the initiatives taken actually move it towards its visionary position.

The other problem is the increased focus on corporate governance. Don't get me wrong: corporate governance is a good thing. But there must be boundaries. The difficulty at the moment is it's become such a large part of a director's job, sometimes at the expense of other more important matters—such as increasing long-term shareholder value.

You can see evidence of this in the proliferation of board sub-committees that deal with audit, remuneration, sustainability etc. Board meeting agendas now overflow with compliance issues—accounting, legal, occupational health and safety, environmental etc. Unfortunately it's turned directors into corporate policemen, which is understandable but arguably not the best use of their time.

The problem lies in the lack of protection directors are given to do their job effectively. When you have directors exposed to personal liability claims if things go wrong, they have no choice but to be extremely cautious.

Furthermore, how can a board that meets for only 12-20 days per year (or less) expect to deal with all these governance issues while still providing the leadership to keep the business on track?

To get everything done, the responsibilities between management and the board must be clearly understood. Each plays a complementary role, but they're not the same. The board must have an excellent overview of the business, but preferably from 3,000 metres up, not from the ground. By staying out of the day-to-day operations a board can offer a unique and valuable perspective, especially around emerging threats and opportunities. They can also lend their specific expertise and wisdom to areas where the company needs help, allowing management to get on with running the company.

Strategic planning is a shared responsibility between the board and management. Management should take the lead on this, but the board should have input and be able to challenge management's view and assumptions. In the end, the aim is to get the best possible plan with the greatest chance of success. Once this is done, any short-term actions taken should be consistent with the long-term vision. And anything that isn't should be closely scrutinised before it's implemented.

The best boards work smoothly and cohesively with management. They supervise and provide guidance without undermining the efforts of the management team. They understand their role precisely, and don't over-step their boundaries. They expect high performance standards, and take action when they don't get it.

Importantly they are vigilant in creating and nurturing an environment to ensure that both good and bad news flows up and down quickly.

Most good boards understand a great CEO is a rare breed. They put their egos aside and appreciate that the CEO is more valuable to the business than they are. A great CEO may view the board as a nuisance but a necessary evil. And this tension is what makes a great relationship. A smart board will give the CEO a lot of rope, but not enough to hang himself. And the CEO will do everything possible to get more rope.

The skill is in getting the balance right.

People Matter

Your people are your business' most precious resource. You might have the best business idea in the world, but you need the right people to make your vision a reality.

But you'll never find out about a person by reading their resume. Some things will become apparent through their actions, while others will stay hidden for as long as they can manage.

The trick is to find the right people for your business, and then do everything you can to keep them. And if someone isn't right for your business, then they'll need to be moved on.

Let The Thoroughbreds Run

Every so often in business you come across someone who's special. Who sees things others don't. Who works that bit harder, and pushes the envelope a bit further. Who takes charge without being asked or prompted.

They're brave, resilient and smart. They want things to work, and will put themselves out there to make it happen. They won't always get it right, and they'll have their share of critics as they push the envelope. It may also get bumpy for them at times, but they don't particularly care.

They're not motivated by winning favour with their bosses or being noticed (although they're usually hard to miss). What's important to them is improvement—both their own and that of the organisation.

I love these people wholeheartedly. They're thoroughbreds—rare and precious. They're born to run, not to be shackled by mediocrity and beaten to death by sacred cows or controlling bosses. It's not in their nature to nod, acquiesce and accept the status quo.

They're genetically coded to find ways to make things better. To solve problems and create opportunities.

Let them.

Give them enough room to be creative. They work best when they're not hemmed in by rules and procedures. But support and mentor them too, because they'll need your help from time to time as they fulfil their potential.

It's well worth the effort.

Mole or Meerkat?

I was once asked whether I was a mole or a meerkat. It was a strange question, and I didn't have a clue what was meant by it. But I was intrigued by it, and started researching the difference between the two animals.

I discovered the mole is a solitary, industrious animal that burrows away underground most of the day looking for food. The mole works alone, avoids others and rarely comes above ground. His only concern is digging and finding food, and is outstanding at both. He lives for about three years.

So a mole works hard, digs all day, avoids contact with other moles and dies young.

Doesn't sound like much fun to me.

Meerkats, on the other hand, are very social and live in colonies with 20-30 members. They're very affectionate, regularly grooming each other to strengthen their social bonds. Meerkats spend all day outdoors, and are often seen scanning their surroundings for opportunities and dangers. They help each other by providing information and insights about what's happening around them.

They play, work and socialise together. They like to wrestle, and have even been seen in what appeared to be foot races.

They live twice as long as moles, and seem to have a lot more fun along the way.

Moles are very useful in business—they're the organisation's workhorses. Give them a pile of work to do and they'll crunch through it day after day, month after month. They like working alone and aren't interested in managing others. Leave them alone and they'll get the job done. They're earnest, reliable and valuable.

But they're not leaders, and their careers will eventually hit a natural ceiling.

Why? Because as you move further up the ladder it's less about your specific skills and how hard you work, and more about how well you can guide, lead, and inspire a team to follow you. It's about getting the best out of your teammates.

And you can't do that working solo, no matter how good you are or how hard you work.

Meerkats work hard too. But they do it in the context of protecting and nurturing their colony, and giving it a chance not just to survive but to prosper.

The same way successful leaders operate.

So am I a mole or a meerkat? I think I'm a meerkat who can do mole-like work when the need arises.

Which one are you?

Simplifiers vs. Complicators

A subset of the moles and meerkats distinction is *simplifiers* and *complicators*.

To understand the difference it's necessary to observe the method used by each of them to solve problems. It all comes down to whether they choose to complicate their approach to the problem or to simplify it.

'Complicators' instinctively reject straightforward, sensible ideas and instead look for more complicated, difficult solutions in most situations.

PowerPoint is their BFF and they default to writing 40 page reports, replete with endless graphs and tables, when a page or two or a phone call will suffice.

They stew over their work for days or weeks invariably missing deadlines and chewing through precious organisational resources. They always seem to lurch from one 'urgent priority' to the next, working long hours regularly as they try to keep up.

Even worse they create progress bottlenecks while their team waits for them to 'become available' and the overall pace of activity slows as a result.

Either out of a fear of failure or a need to demonstrate intelligence they repeat this doomed approach for years on end until they either burn out or get kicked out.

Along the way they alienate and exhaust their team who give up trying to keep up. Worst still the complicator is oblivious to all of this and considers their own behaviour/approach normal and rational.

'Simplifiers' on the other hand are adept at getting to the heart of an issue quickly without fuss or fanfare.

Even for complex tasks they understand how to synthesise data into easy to understand insights that solve problems expediently.

They write short reports and communicate complicated ideas effectively and well with their team to ensure that everyone's knowledge increases as a result of their work.

They don't complain about being busy, don't waste time on things that are trivial or unnecessary and importantly they ensure that they never bottleneck progress.

While moles, meerkats and simplifiers are all useful to organisations, complicators never are and I have little patience with them. They get in the way of progress and that slows things down.

And that's bad for business.

The Best Behavioural Trait In Business...

If I had to nominate a behavioural trait that separates the best people from everyone else, it would have to be that the best people treat company money as if it is their own money. At every decision point they ask themselves, "If this was my own money, would I spend it like this?"

It doesn't always happen. In fact many people have a loose, even blasé attitude towards spending company money. Here are a few examples I've seen over the years:

- One person I know collects restaurant receipts (not his) and claims them as entertainment expenses.
- Another person likes to stay in expensive hotels, which his company doesn't allow. So he gets his local manager to pay his accommodation bill, and then authorises the payment himself to avoid his boss seeing it.
- Another guy claims work boots as a company expense, even though he's actually buying expensive dress shoes.

Other people 'steal time' by showing up late, leaving early, being unproductive and distracting other team members. And even more people use company assets for personal use, 'borrowing' an item or two out of the stock, stationery or sample room.

It's okay if they ask permission first. But if they don't, then it's no different to stealing. What's really bad is some people justify to themselves that this type of behaviour is acceptable. Some even believe they're entitled to it. Or worse, deserve it.

One lesson I learnt a long time ago is that, whether it's in business or in life, you're entitled to nothing and don't deserve anything. To get what you want you have to do the hard work and pay your dues. No shortcuts.

And if you don't understand that, you'll have a hard time reaching your full potential.

A few years ago I visited one of my employees at home, and noticed he had a large supply of our company shelving in his back shed. I asked him what it was doing there, and whether he got permission to take it from the company premises. He brushed it off, saying it was "surplus to company requirements".

To make a point, I wheeled his brand new lawn mower out to my four-wheel drive and started loading it into the back. He watched with his mouth wide open, then tentatively asked what I was doing. I told him he seemed to have a fluid attitude towards ownership of company and personal assets, that the company needed a new lawn mower, and that this one would be perfect.

He got the point.

A team that treats company money like their own is the Holy Grail of business. A prize to be nurtured, developed and protected. Building a business with a team like this is a fun, gratifying, and ultimately profitable experience.

... And The Worst Behavioural Traits In Business

This was hard for me to write because I had to dredge through some bad memories of people I've worked with that I'd rather forget. But here goes:

- **Dishonesty.** Dishonest people think they're smarter than you. They try to gain the advantage through deceit or duplicity. They don't do what they say they'll do, and will invent a million reasons why it's someone else's fault when things go wrong.
- **Superiority.** These people look down their nose at others. They have huge egos, and believe they're owed respect whether they've earned it or not. Many have fragile personalities and aren't nearly as good as they think they are. They hide behind big job titles and are easily impressed by other people's wealth and status. They enjoy power for all the wrong reasons, and don't like being challenged because it might expose their own vulnerabilities.
- **Narcissism.** The narcissist is always seeking attention. They lack empathy, and feign human emotions such as compassion and humility. But their actions always make it clear they only care about themselves.
- **Fence sitting.** Fence sitters value self-interest above everything else. They live in constant fear of doing something wrong and losing some privilege they currently enjoy. They avoid responsibility, and won't make a decision unless forced to. Even then they'll carefully consider how it will affect them personally. These people are usually fine when

everything's going smoothly, but completely useless when things get rough.

- Closely aligned with fence sitters are those who just **go through the motions**. These people want the rewards without the work. They tell you what you want to hear. They'll do the minimum, talk themselves up, but constantly under-perform. To deflect attention or criticism they feign confusion and misunderstanding. And despite never fully engaging themselves in the business, they'll complain about being under-valued and blame others for their lack of career progress.

- **Johnny-come-lately**. These people arrive at a workplace, look around for a month and then declare everything is wrong and they have all the answers. In their minds they're the saviours, but they're actually naïve and dangerous. They talk a lot, and pretend to listen. Ignoring history they'll quickly form views and construct plans based on rudimentary facts and research. And they all want to make their mark in the first three months. They usually screw up.

These behaviours aren't mutually exclusive. I've known people who had more than one. But they were all toxic influences in the business, and had to be shown the door.

There was no other choice.

(If you *really* want to understand someone in your business, talk to the people who report to them. Chances are they'll have the most accurate view.)

The Ultimate Feedback Question

For many people, dealing with constructive criticism is very difficult. While they're happy to accept praise, they find it extremely tough to deal with negative feedback. Norman Vincent Peale once said, "The trouble with most of us is that we'd rather be ruined by praise than saved by criticism".

He may be right.

I observed this situation first-hand at a company I was advising. Whenever the CEO received any criticism he just shut down. He couldn't cope with it, and wouldn't do anything about it. He just didn't want to be told what to do.

He couldn't believe his team's perception of him was entirely different to his own. He never bothered asking anyone for their view, and no-one bothered to tell him. When I pointed this out he froze and went into denial. His ego had been severely bruised.

The problem is some successful people are actually delusional about their achievements and abilities. When times are good they take the credit, but when they're bad they blame others. They may have been stellar performers in the past, but their success has made them lazy, complacent and out of touch. They don't like being told they're wrong, and they don't want to change no matter how compelling the evidence is.

Unfortunately, their self-worth is too closely associated with their position, so they take negative feedback personally and ignore the facts. US Statesman Colin Powell provided great advice when he said, "Avoid having your ego so close to your position that when your position falls, your ego goes with it." And "Listen to everything said. If you don't believe it, say so. But do it without being defensive. If you are proved wrong say so. Then do something about it. That builds trust."

What you need to understand is you'll always have critics as well as admirers, and you should treat criticism and praise in exactly the same way—clinically, open-mindedly and quickly. If it's valuable to your end-goals (and that includes becoming better and more effective), then use it. If not, then ignore it.

The key is to search for the truth in any criticism.

Feedback is always about past issues and behaviours. You can't change the past, so focus on what you can do about the future instead. If you get any feedback (negative or positive), don't argue about it or defend it. Instead ask this simple question: "How can I do better?" It defuses almost any situation and cuts to the heart of the problem. Even better, it focuses on the solution instead of the problem.

Next time someone gives you feedback, try it out. The power of this simple question in influencing culture and performance might surprise you.

Know Your 'Use by Date'

I've never spent more than seven years in an organisation. The average is about four. Any longer and I'm 'cooked'—tired, burnt out and bored. There's also a good chance I'll start doing the things I *like* to do instead of what the organisation *needs* me to do, which isn't good for anyone. So I move on, and hand over the reins to someone who can bring in new ideas, perspectives and energy.

It's fortunate that I understand my 'use by date' and the patterns of behaviour as I approach it. It helps keep me fresh and motivated.

Not sure if you're approaching your use by date? Here are some signs to watch out for:

- You lack passion, and are simply going through the motions.
- Your energy levels are low and you're always tired.
- You dabble and micro-manage, and you focus on the present instead of the future.
- You avoid contact with your staff, suppliers and customers whenever you can.
- You say "We tried that before and it didn't work" regularly, and blame others when things go wrong.
- Your personal interests consume more and more of your business time, and you avoid business travel or field trips.

And at the organisational level, your team will be heard saying things like:

- "We have to make it sound like it's the boss' idea or he won't agree with it."
- "There's no point trying to do this—the boss will never agree."

In the end the good people leave because they can no longer make a difference. And the bad ones stay, perpetuating the status quo.

A CEO or senior executive who doesn't recognise these warning signs is dangerous from both a cultural and financial perspective. Leaders like this are typically running organisations that are stuck in the past and resistant to change, with high staff turnover and low morale. It's impossible for an organisation to think strategically in these circumstances, and that makes it vulnerable.

Knowing your use by date, and departing gracefully when you reach it, is an acquired skill. It might be more comfortable to stay but ultimately it will end badly unless you can rediscover your passion and drive. That's tough to do in an organisation where you have history, however, and is often easier somewhere else where you can come in fresh and re-invigorated.

So be brave, move on, and create a new path. It's far better than suddenly being forced to leave, invariably described as "leaving to pursue other opportunities", but really meaning that you've outlived your welcome and breached your use by date.

Don't Accept Praise You Don't Deserve

One of the quirks of business (and the human condition in general) is when something goes well, anyone remotely attached to it will try to claim credit for it. And of course, when the poo hits the fan most people will conveniently vanish and blame someone else.

I have a real issue with people accepting undeserved praise or credit for something they didn't do. It's short-sighted, and a quick way to devalue yourself in the eyes of your team. Maybe they do it because they have low IQ, EQ or self-esteem. Perhaps they're blinded by their own ambition or self-interest. Or they might be so eager to get a pat on the back from their 'masters' they don't care whether they actually deserved it.

Whatever the case, it's fake and dishonest. And that's never good.

Instead, share praise and recognition fully and transparently. Make sure everyone knows where the credit really sits, and broadcast it widely and loudly. Don't fudge your own achievements—you'll get found out eventually.

The best people I know understand it's better to take a little more of the blame when things go wrong, and a little less of the credit when things go well. They also know you'll get a lot more done if you don't care who gets the credit.

But what's the payoff for this type of behaviour? It builds loyalty, and this protects the giver when times get rough. Why? Because they know the more credit they give away, the more it will find its way back to them. They also know the more they acknowledge and help their team, the more their team will want to help them.

It's simple karma.

You Get What You Tolerate

One of the hardest things to do in business is to let people go. It's never an enjoyable task, and most of us will have a few sleepless nights building up to it. We'll debate with ourselves about whether it's easier to persevere with them and hope they change, and even justify why they really aren't as bad as we think.

We delay the decision and time rolls on. The person doesn't improve, which makes us even more frustrated.

Eventually the problem becomes so big there's no other choice but to move them on.

Many 'failures' occur because the person trusted to get the job done comes up short. While it's important to give them a second chance to prove themselves, patience of this type has its limits. A poor attitude makes it a lot easier to move them along without delay. But if there's a disconnection in expectations then you should try to line them up before taking more drastic action.

The saddest situation is when people with great attitudes who try really hard just aren't good enough.

As Albert Einstein famously put it, "Insanity is continuing to do the same thing over and over again and expecting to get a different result". The same logic applies to expecting staff members to perform at a higher level than they're willing or able to do.

For an organisation to succeed in the long run, its 'gene pool' needs refreshing periodically—moving some people on, adjusting some roles, and introducing some new (outside) talent to bring in new skills and experience. It's an evolutionary process that's necessary to stay ahead of the pack.

Or you can decide to do nothing. In which case you'll get what you tolerate.

But you probably won't like it.

Important note: Firing someone from their job is often a catastrophic event for them. Never do it lightly or with limited information, and make sure you're empathetic with your approach. If you honestly believe they can reach the performance level required, then give them every chance to improve. Coach them, encourage them, and make your expectations clear. But act decisively and with compassion if it doesn't work out.

Surviving And Prospering In A Large Corporation

A good friend of mine is a corporate survivor, having worked in big businesses his entire career. Despite restructures, retrenchments and mergers, he's inched his way to the top and made a lot of money along the way.

He's a quiet guy with a steely resolve. He isn't a workaholic, and enjoys a good work-life balance. He doesn't check email or answer his phone on the weekends. As far as he's concerned that time is for family and friends—no-one else.

But when he works he's totally switched on and goes at 100 miles per hour.

Speaking to him, it's obvious he cares about doing the right thing for the company. He never criticises it or any of his workmates. In his mind they all have a job to do, and as a leader he has to set the right example. He does his best to avoid corporate politics, and treats everyone the same way no matter who they are.

Recently his company restructured its operations, and many of his peers lost their jobs. But he didn't. In fact, he was promoted. And it's not first time it's happened.

I asked him what the secret was to not only his survival but also his success. He modestly said that the more self-reliant you are, and the less support you need to successfully operate, the further you'll go and the more valuable you'll be to an organisation.

He told me he's never had a PA despite all his peers having one, and rarely outsources work. The tighter he can run things the better. It forces him to focus on doing the big things well—things that create real value for his organisation.

With a 'worker' ethos running through his veins, every minute is precious to him. He prioritises well and doesn't get involved in anything that will waste his time or distract him from his objectives.

He minimises downtime well. You won't find him having long lunches or sitting in a corporate box at the football. He hates travelling, and reduces his time away by getting an early flight out and a late flight home. To him, time is more important than comfort.

On the outside he's humble and modest. But underneath it all he has absolute confidence in himself. He's very good at what he does, and produces better results with fewer resources than his peers.

If his company wants something done, difficult or otherwise, he's the guy they turn to. It makes him extremely valuable. Not indispensable, but damn close to it.

And that's why he doesn't just survive in big business— he prospers.

Compare this to a guy who worked for me back in the late 1990s who I had to let go because of poor performance.

When I told him this he responded with - 'You're making the worst decision of your life. Letting me go will cripple this company. You can't operate without me, as you'll soon discover. You're screwed, mate.'

He headed up a small team in another country that contributed nearly 20% of the company's total revenue and earnings, and was an important growth engine in our future plans. It wasn't a simple or easy decision for me.

But I didn't trust him anymore. He'd become slack, and while he talked a good game the business' performance was declining. Worst still, he thought his behaviour had passed unnoticed. He was operating on the 'out of sight and out of mind' principle, but it was all a house of cards that eventually collapsed on him.

Still, he was correct with one of his assertions. Within a month all the other employees either resigned or were fired, leaving us with the headache of operating a business with no staff.

We were crippled.

I immediately shut the doors, and redirected all phone numbers, email addresses and mail to our Australian office. I also sent two members of our senior team over to talk to suppliers and customers, and explain how we intended to restructure the business.

For five months we ran the business without a local presence. But in that time business actually got better. Eventually we pieced together what had happened under the previous regime.

It wasn't good.

He'd created a lazy, complacent environment where he worked from 10 till 2 at best, with the rest of the team playing follow the leader. The signs were all there, but we'd either missed or ignored them.

So we started again. Within six months we established a brand new team, and the business hasn't looked back since. It's an experience I wouldn't want to repeat too often, but it was the right decision (even if it did result in some serious short-term pain).

It's easy to think a business can't run without you. It's even easier to give yourself too much credit for what's been achieved. No-one is irreplaceable, and it's a fair bet there's someone out there who's better than you.

Companies don't care whether you're replaceable or not because they know most people are. What they want is fairly simple—consistently good work and a great attitude.

And if you really want to go places then you'll need to be able to do the following:

- Recognise and uncover good opportunities.
- Influence others to follow you.
- Manage implementation to ensure it works while containing the downside risks
- Get it done with limited resources.

How successful you are in doing this will ultimately determine your worth to an organisation. And, although no-one is irreplaceable, some people are a hell of a lot more valuable than others.

The trick is to keep moving up the list.

How To 'Manage Up'

Here's one of business' 'plain truths': Unless you can effectively 'manage up' you'll probably never reach your full potential or achieve everything you otherwise might.

One of my mentors gave me that advice twenty years ago, and he was absolutely right. But how do you do it?

Start by putting yourself in the shoes of those you report to so you can understand what they want. They're usually time-poor, and quickly need to believe you're in charge and 'have it covered'. They need clear signs that this is true. If they don't see any they'll get nervous, meddle more and start making decisions for you instead of letting you get on with it.

In the end it's all about confidence. And the more confident they are about you, the more room they'll give you to operate.

To do that you need to set clear, joint behavioural and performance expectations up front. Have a clear plan that they support, and then provide regular updates on your progress. To start with I suggest sending them a brief written report every week outlining key data and insights they can digest in two or three minutes. Then follow it up with a phone call or face-to-face meeting if necessary.

This will minimise surprises, and bring order and predictability to the relationship. It will also ensure everyone has the most up-to-date information possible.

Of course, this doesn't replace the more formal reporting requirements. It just provides a more timely flow of key information and encourages more regular communication. This will free up more management and board time to spend on value-accretive activities instead of being 'brought up to date'.

It also doesn't hurt to *test the temperature* of the relationship periodically by proactively asking for performance feedback from your boss, rather than waiting around for your scheduled performance review.

Shrinking violets don't win the confidence of senior managers, directors or investors. You should always be gracious and open, but you also need to be firm. Have a view that's supported by insights, data and experience. Talk in plain English about what's *really* going on, and how you plan to manage the risks and opportunities going forward. If things aren't going well you need to quickly tell the truth, but always have a plan to turn things around even if it isn't fully formed. And if things *are* going well, let them know you haven't taken your foot off the accelerator by showing them solid plans to stretch your success even further.

And whatever else you do set yourself high personal standards of behaviour and performance and do your best to live up to them.

Remember: the people above you want to trust you. After all, they probably appointed you in the first place. They want it to work, and for you to succeed. When good people are involved, it's usually all they want. They'll be on your side until your lose their confidence.

Don't let that happen.

The Secret of Job Contentment

I know a lot of people who don't like their jobs.

Or their bosses.

Some believe they're under-paid and under-appreciated, and are frustrated their career progress doesn't match their own aspirations. Others envy their peers and colleagues who seem to be doing better than they are.

Sound familiar?

The answer may lie in how they define their own happiness and contentment. They probably line up for their annual performance review hoping they'll be rewarded with more money, more opportunities, and the benefits they think they're entitled to.

And therein lies the problem. The boss is just another cog in the machine, often with a limited capacity to influence much and constrained by budgets and pressure from their own boss. They may (or may not) be trying their best, but come up short because the pool is too small to satisfy everyone.

At this point it's easy to get frustrated and resentful. But what does it achieve? It doesn't get you what you want. And the problem may be as much with you as it is with the organisation.

So what can you do? Here are a couple of options:

Leave.

If it's that unbearable, go and get a job somewhere else (or maybe even start your own business). It could be better, or you could find yourself just as frustrated in a year or two.

What *actually* happens will depend on your attitude. Which brings us to the second option.

Get happy.

Huh?

Yes, I'm serious. Start getting happy where you are, with whatever you have. And focus on what you have, rather than worrying and fretting about what you *don't* have.

Then commit yourself to producing great work that's important and valuable. Work that's fun, and that you love doing. Work that makes you happy where you are or wherever you decide to go. Work that solves real problems, and gets you noticed and rewarded.

You might think I'm over-simplifying a complex matter. But in the end there *are* only two options—stay or leave—and the choice will be different for everyone.

My point is, don't let your attitude hold you back. A poor attitude and an aura of resentment *will* get you noticed, but it won't do much for your job satisfaction or future prospects.

Getting happy and producing important and valuable work you love doing. Maybe *that's* the key to job contentment. If nothing else it will make working a lot more fun. And you *will* be favourably noticed—guaranteed. Eventually you may have companies walking over hot coals to hire or retain you, and even engaging you if you break out on your own.

Staying Sharp

Managing a business isn't easy. There's so much to manage—people, processes, finances, operations and so on. And sometimes dealing with one can upset another.

Fortunately there are tools, techniques and strategies you can use to get on top of everything and make it all run smoothly.

Or at least smoother than it was before.

Stop, Start, Continue

The term 'continuous improvement' gets used a lot in business. For some organisations it just creates a lot of 'busy' work that doesn't achieve very much. But for others it becomes a deeply embedded discipline that relentlessly drives the business forward.

Continuous improvement is about staying ahead of your competitors by constantly looking for small, incremental improvements that continuously add value. And one of the better methods of extracting value from continuous improvement is the STOP, START, CONTINUE strategy. It can be used at any level of an organisation, and applied anywhere from high-level strategic matters to how an individual does their job.

You start with crystal clear objectives—knowing what you're trying to achieve, and by when. Here's how it works:

1. **STOP** doing anything that doesn't move you towards your objectives. Cut old processes, uncommercial deals, 'dead wood' in your team, etc. These are holding you back from a brighter future and you need to stop them, no matter how painful it is to do.

2. **START** doing activities that will help you achieve your objectives more quickly. Pivot if you need to. Introduce new initiatives the market wants and will pay for. Upgrade your team with people who give a damn. Start giving your customers and suppliers more care and love. Hit every deadline and budget you get. Run faster and harder, now that you're free of the baggage you cut away in the STOP phase.

3.   **CONTINUE** doing the things you're doing well. The good stuff. The stuff that's 'bang on' in terms of meeting your business and cultural objectives. And if you can, do more of it.

The STOP, START, CONTINUE ethos provides a way to regularly recalibrate a business, job or project and keep it lined up against its set objectives. It can help an organisation get rid of the bad practices, clutter and noise that get in the way of progress. If an activity or behaviour doesn't help move the business forward, it goes. If it does, it stays. And if new things are needed to enhance progress, they get started.

Perhaps the key is to 'do less, better'—to do a small number of things really well and shut down everything else?

Business Isn't A Point-To-Point Race

Staying nimble is more important than ever as markets change and evolve rapidly. You can quickly become redundant or obsolete unless you are alert to emerging opportunities and risks. It doesn't hurt too to keep an eye on your competitors and attack them when they are at their most vulnerable.

Here is a personal story about how I outwitted a much stronger opponent by staying nimble and keeping him guessing. While not a business story it nevertheless shows what can be achieved if you keep your eyes and ears open to tactical opportunities that emerge unexpectedly.

Twice a week for ten years straight I headed to Elwood Beach on Melbourne's foreshore at 7am to spend time with a group of my friends being tortured by our personal trainer.

One guy I trained with goes by the nickname 'The Greyhound'. He's a few years younger (and 15 kilos lighter) than I am, a better all-round athlete and a top bloke to boot.

He's also fast (he once ran a marathon in under three hours), and on a straight point-to-point sprint race he wins easily no matter how hard I try.

But things get a bit more interesting when there's an obstacle in the way and he can no longer rely on his straight-out speed.

On one memorable occasion I won all three of our sprint races for the first time ever. It's all in the name of fun, but we're both competitive and still enjoy holding bragging rights over each other.

It all happened 35 minutes into our session, after being flogged to near exhaustion by our trainer. The course is an unusual one—a 40-metre straight section, a 90-degree left turn, a short 15-metre straight section, another 90-degree left turn, and a final 15-metre sprint to the finish line.

It's tough.

In the first race we ambled to the start line and I caught the greyhound napping, getting away to a fast start. I led by ten metres heading into the first corner, and won comfortably.

The second race was different. The Greyhound waited for another fast start from me. But he didn't get —I let him lead and sat on his right shoulder. Just before the first corner I accelerated in front of him, forcing him to the outside and slowing him down. I held my speed at the short straight and the next turn, and cruised home in front.

In the third race I played possum. I told The Greyhound I was happy to win two out of three races. I said it should be an easy victory for him because I had no energy left.

When the race started I hung back and let him lead. "I'm cooked," I called out. He eased off, and I caught him by surprise by accelerating hard. He wasn't expecting it, and I opened up a three-metre lead. I hung onto it through the two main turns, and won by a few metres.

The Greyhound's strength is his natural speed and running ability, honed by years of practice. Mine is being able to stop and start quickly and maintain my speed around the turns, honed by 20 years of playing rugby.

But what got me over the line that day were the tactics I employed. If I'd just 'pinned my ears back' and relied on pure speed he would have beaten me easily. I didn't have the legs to take The 'Hound that way. And I wouldn't have won if I'd broadcast my moves in advance. Instead I kept him guessing by changing my tactics, which caught him off guard and allowed me to sneak home three times.

Business isn't a point-to-point race either. It's an unscripted journey, and where you end up depends heavily on being able to hold your nerve and make sensible decisions every day—even when you have incomplete information (which may be most of the time).

Having a deep understanding of your competitors and where they're vulnerable certainly helps. If they're large, powerful and well-resourced then a 'storm the fort' approach probably won't work—they'll squash you.

You're better off finding a weakness you can exploit and focusing on that. (It also doesn't hurt to turn yourself into a moving target that's difficult for them to hit.)

In his book *The Art of War,* Chinese philosopher Sun Tzu wrote, "If your enemy is secure at all points, be prepared for him. If he is in superior strength, evade him. If your opponent is temperamental, seek to irritate him. Pretend to be weak so that he grows arrogant. If he is taking his ease, give him no rest. If his forces are united, separate them. If sovereign and subject are in accord, put division between them. Attack him where he is unprepared, appear where you are not expected".

That's good advice. War and business are very similar. They both rely on one simple objective—beating your competition. And doing so ensures your survival.

There's also little point in publicly criticising your competition. Instead capitalise on their vulnerabilities by highlighting your own points of difference, and explain how they translate into hard-to-find customer benefits. Then systematically execute as if your life depended on it.

And one last thing - if you ever come across a competitor who is doing it tough (or *drowning)* take the advice of Ray Kroc, founder of McDonalds, and stick a hose in their mouth.

Then go after their customers.

The Optimal Operating Speed

I often ask myself if there's an optimal operating speed for businesses, and what that speed might be. Is it best to pin your ears back and take on a lot at once? Work at a slow, cautious, more methodical pace? Or do something in between?

It's a perplexing question, and I still don't think I have the answer. I *do* think there's an optimal speed for businesses to run at, but it's different for each one.

The best speed, in my view, is to go as fast as you can without losing control. That is, be driven by urgency to get things done but don't move faster than your underlying ability to successfully execute what you want to do.

This is the concept of making slow haste.

The intersection point, the fastest speed possible moderated by the internal capability to successfully execute your plans, is the sweet spot of slow haste and arguably the optimal speed for businesses to operate at.

This means that no matter how long your to-do list is, or how urgent things seem, you must be able to ingest (and more importantly embed) these initiatives before moving on to the next item on your list.

You need sufficient capacity in your structure and your team to oversee and manage anything new. You also need a strong set of business rules (i.e. principles and values) in place to govern the organisation's behaviour, and rock-solid processes and procedures that let you get things done quickly without having to reinvent the wheel every time there's something new.

These rules and procedures are critical to maintaining speed within a business. No matter how good you think you might be, if your plans out-pace your capacity to execute them you'll break your team and create frustration. And if you move too slowly you'll risk boredom, miss opportunities, and expose yourself to more aggressive competition.

In the end, ideas are cheap and readily available. What's less common is the ability to successfully execute those ideas and turn them into something important and meaningful. The key is to understand your internal capabilities, and know what you can sensibly do within a certain timeframe. The next step is to take deliberate action. But always remember not to exceed slow haste— your optimal operating speed.

Create Replicable Operating Systems

It isn't easy for a business to get traction, especially in the early days. It's even harder to scale and succeed in the long term. One crucial element is to create replicable operating systems that allow the business to work without the person at the top doing everything themselves.

McDonalds is a classic example of a business with rock-solid operating procedures and systems that underpin its capacity to innovate and grow. McDonalds is obsessive about training its people to ensure consistency in every store it operates. It has a detailed operations manual that's several thousand pages long and covers everything that could possibly happen or go wrong.

They've effectively standardised their operations so any function can be completed by people with the lowest possible level of skill needed for it. If someone is away, then the next person can easily step into the role and do the job. This seamless approach has allowed McDonalds to franchise their operations worldwide and enjoy enormous success.

Business works best when an integrated operating system is developed to run the business. People then run the system. The trick is to standardise as much as you can to reduce the need for ongoing higher-level human intervention. What we're really talking about is 'dumbing down' your business to make your output system-dependent (rather than people-dependent) as much as possible. Just remember that your system must also meet the needs of your customers.

To properly systemise a business you need to document everything you do. Every policy and procedure needs to be explained in a way that's predictable and easy to follow. And the measure of success is whether everybody does the same thing the same way every time. It shouldn't matter if someone is away—anyone should be able to learn the systems quickly so there's minimum disruption to the business. The great thing about documented systems is that when they're followed they produce consistent, predictable results.

Systems are great. They give you more time to work *on* the business, not *in* the business. But keep a close eye on whether you're getting the results you want from your efforts. If you're not, parts of the system may need to be changed. Don't fret about it—it's quite normal. It may even take some periodical reinvention to get it working properly.

One last thing: Never consider your systems and processes as being complete. They're always a work in progress, and need constant development as your business grows. They shouldn't be set in stone.

The Things That Don't Scale

The ultimate achievement for most business builders and entrepreneurs is to build a large-scale enterprise that changes markets and people's lives while making a ton of money. It's a great end-game, and some businesses have actually achieved it.

But most businesses start very differently. They start by doing things that don't scale. Things their larger competitors have trouble copying. Things that set them apart, and give them a discernible competitive differentiation and advantage. Things that can't be scaled by technology, or adding more people to a call centre. Things that bind their customers and suppliers to them.

This is more than just providing good customer service or occasionally buying a key customer lunch. It's about letting them inside the doors of your business to understand your aspirations and challenges. Drawing them into your team as allies.

This lesson was driven home to me during the early days of Calendar Club. I was leasing retail sites from a major Australian shopping centre developer, and having an incredibly tough time doing it. The relationship was confrontational, but the equation was simple. They wanted as much rent as they could get every year, and I wanted to pay as little as possible. It wasn't working for me, and I needed to change tactics.

So I looked for an ally within the largest developer group. Someone I could work with who would hopefully be interested in helping to develop the business and fight internal battles for us within his organisation. I eventually found him too (after discarding a couple of duds along the way).

The relationship took a long time to develop as we worked each other out. But bit by bit the trust began to build. I had to let him sensibly 'inside our tent' and show him our inner workings—not an easy thing to do. But I grew to trust him, and he never betrayed that trust in more than ten years. In fact he told me that over time he grew to admire the business and what we'd achieved, especially starting with few resources and limited cash. He felt that he was part of that success, and he was. It was also a win-win situation because he built a growing rent book off the back of our ability to open more sites each year.

Looking back on our long association I could not have found a better ally. And the business certainly wouldn't have grown to the size or scale it did without his help. It wasn't a scalable relationship (it needed both of us to work) but it had a huge impact on our ability to scale the business in subsequent years.

Many other (now) successful companies shared similar early-stage *non-scaling* experiences in their efforts to gain market traction.

Seek is an example. Today Seek is the market leader in online job advertising in Australasia with a market capitalisation of nearly A$5bn. But back when it started in 1997 it was a minnow attempting to take on the entrenched media behemoths that dominated employment advertising via their newspapers and who had enjoyed an unchallenged run for decades.

Like most start-ups Seek was under-resourced and probably under-funded. But the three founders were determined and smart guys. Legend has it that they would have their customers fax them their job ads for the Saturday papers and they would personally sit up all night typing the ads into their website.

Online retailer Catch of the Day grew out of a homespun eBay store and in their early days the founders drove the streets of suburban Melbourne door-knocking companies trying to source cheap, surplus stock that they could on-sell through their burgeoning site.

No matter what your business does or how mature it is, you need to pay close attention to not only the things that will scale, but also the things critical to your future success that *won't* scale. They can get you started and/or give you that competitive edge you've been looking for. In my case I got smoother access to something I really needed (reasonably priced sites in shopping centres). It's usually hard work and takes a personal touch and that alone makes it difficult to copy or scale.

But I guess that's the point. It's hard for good reason, and many people will avoid doing it. But those who do know one truth— sometimes the things that don't scale are the *only* things that will help you eventually scale in the future.

The Scoop Guy

In every business I've managed for the past twenty years, I was a 'scoop guy'. It's not a popular role (I certainly didn't ask for it), and it's not well understood either. But every business needs one.

Essentially the scoop guy *expects* things to go wrong, and works out where the likely problems and pressure points will be in advance. He puts processes in place to stop most of them happening, and then "scoops up" the ones that fall through the cracks before they hit the floor and become major issues.

The scoop guy understands that if a problem happens more than once it's probably systemic, and a process must be installed immediately to ensure it doesn't happen again. He hates surprises, and will do whatever he can to minimise them as much as possible. He knows that stopping problems from occurring will give the organisation more time to work on initiatives that really matter.

But while the role of the scoop guy isn't glamorous, a good one can create a lot of value for a company.

Central to this approach is making sure bad news travels fast in an organisation. I like good news as much as the next person, and I'm usually the first one to celebrate it. But I do it quickly and then move on. The past is the past, and it can't be altered. The future is less predictable, and so I'm far more interested in hearing about bad news and problems first.

You can't fix problems you don't know about. So the scoop guy actively seeks out problems, gathers facts quickly and then takes decisive action. He knows there's no steady-state in business, and that small issues can escalate quickly if left unattended or unresolved.

Compare this with other organisations that shy away from conflict, disappointment, or making hard or unpopular decisions. They either ignore the bad news or hide it, and hope a miracle will save the day. (It rarely does.) Instead it leads to unnecessary delays that amplify the problem and make it much harder to fix later on.

Keep your eyes and ears open, and encourage people to pass on news of any type. But never blame them for things that go wrong. It will quickly shut down the flow of information that's critical to future progress.

And finally, never underestimate the value of a good scoop guy in your organisation. If you've got one, hold on to them. They're hard to find, and worth their weight in gold.

The Life Of A Stripper

Sometimes I shake my head at how seemingly noisy, complex and confused the world has become. We're bombarded with information and stimuli from every angle. The Internet connects us with the world 24/7. We can download movies from home, order a pizza from our TV and run a global business from our phone. We can even join Justin Bieber's 60 million Twitter followers and track his every move if we're so inclined. Isn't it wonderful?

I'm starting to wonder if the trick is not getting caught up in the puffery of it all, and only participating in activities that give you *real* additional value.

That's the art of stripping—to strip out activities, processes, products, services and anything else that uses time and/or resources without producing a valuable result.

But there's one critical distinction that's at the heard of stripping: strippers deal in solving problems, not creating opportunities. They look for real problems to solve—inefficient markets, unsatisfied customer groups, etc. They're far less concerned about developing something sexy and cool, or looking for the next big thing. They're very disciplined and efficient. If what they're doing doesn't solve a genuine problem they'll drop it and move on. And while great opportunities may emerge from their work, strippers know it only happened because a real problem was solved in the process.

Strippers use plain English, and ask far more questions than most people. They assume nothing, and keep digging until they unearth the core of any problem. Along the way they push aside obstacles, smokescreens and entrenched behaviours to get to the truth of any matter. They're constantly cataloguing, discarding and rating the importance of everything they uncover. In the end they're looking for the root cause(s) of the underlying problem in its purest, uncensored state. Only then will they start figuring out how to solve it.

And they do that by asking three simple questions:

- What specific problem are we solving?
- If we solve it will the result be valuable for our target audience?
- Do we need to do it now?

The Aldi grocery chain is a great example of a stripper. They know what they're good at, and they stay focused on it. Their brand message is clear and unambiguous. They're also disciplined. One example is their tight product range, which never exceeds 1,000 items. They regularly introduce new products into their stores, but when they do they remove existing products from the range to make room. Competition for shelf space is high, and every product's financial return is scrutinised and analysed. If there's a better financial option for that shelf space, that product is removed and replaced with the new one. It's classic stripper behaviour.

Strippers like to keep things simple. They know the world is complex, so they focus on de-constructing difficult matters into bite-sized problems they can progressively solve. They efficiently fight their way through waste, confusion and clutter with a single-minded purpose: to solve real problems that will ultimately create value instead of noise for an appreciative and hopefully large audience.

That's the life of a stripper.

The Best-Prepared Guy In The Room

When I was in my 20s I worked for a merchant bank. I started as a Credit Analyst assessing business loan applications, but was soon promoted to management level. This was the heady days of the 1980s, and a revolving door of entrepreneurs, charlatans and business people were beating a path to our offices for funding.

But although I didn't know at the time, I was completely out of my depth.

While I was technically smart enough for the role, I was nowhere near worldly enough. I hadn't yet developed the bullshit detector I rely on so heavily nowadays. I mostly believed what people told me, and made decisions based on an optimistic view of the circumstances presented.

Then one day in 1989, a large syndicated loan to build an office complex in downtown Melbourne changed that forever.

The complex needed $250m in funding, and our bank was proposing to provide $10m of it. To me the deal was a no-brainer—a good developer and strong leasing pre-commitments, with the completion underwritten by a reputable finance company. So I presented the deal to our credit committee, expecting a rubber stamp of approval.

Instead I got shot down in flames.

One committee member was an experienced property guy (an ex-COO of one of Australia's big four banks) and he grilled me relentlessly about the credentials of the builder/developer, the state of the Melbourne office market, and a myriad of other transaction risks I'd only paid cursory attention to. He kept asking me why I thought it was such a great deal. I'd reply as best as I could, and he'd explain to me what I had missed.

Two years later he was proven right when the deal imploded.

After the meeting he pulled me aside, and we had a long chat. He told me that if I wanted to succeed I needed to be better prepared, dig deeper to uncover the real risks, anticipate questions and objections in advance, and generally research more and speculate less. At one point he smiled and said, "Son, I've had a very long and successful career because I always aimed to be the best-prepared guy in the room".

His advice struck me like a thunderbolt. I've never forgotten it, and it's been a bedrock principle for how I've operated ever since. In times of uncertainty it's given me some protection from calamities occurring. It's kept the number of 'surprises' I encounter low. And it's stopped me speculating and providing opinions unless they're well thought through.

(Needless to say I don't use the words "I reckon" much anymore.)

Why Everyone Should Spend Time Working In A Call Centre

If you want to learn about the problems in a business, spend two days working in the call centre.

It's a raw experience. You're quickly bombarded with what customers think of your business—good and bad. Most of all, you learn what they *don't* want.

Some are obvious. Waiting 20 minutes in a call queue sucks. So does out of stock products. Ditto for broken web links. Late deliveries? Not good. Inaccurate billing? Unpopular. Making excuses? Nobody cares.

Sitting in a call centre with headphones on is far less sexy than strategy sessions, media briefings, new product launches or the latest market offer. But it's just as important. Existing customers are the bread and butter of any organisation. They're hard to get, easy to disappoint and difficult to replace. You need to keep them happy.

You need to know what your customers are thinking and what's important to them. Regular stints on the shop floor, in the call centre or on the road with your sales reps are a good way to start. Systematically scouring online forums, blogs, Facebook, etc. will also help. The key is to ask whoever you come into contact with, "What can we do better?"

Even small things that seem trivial—such as a slow-loading web site—could inconvenience customers and cost sales.

In the early days of Amazon, founder Jeff Bezos would bring an empty chair into team meetings to represent the voice of the customer. Nowadays, the company has specially trained 'Customer Service Bar Raisers' who are fanatical about improving customer service.

And when they're not happy, everybody at Amazon knows about it.

If you want to find out the truth about your organisation, head over to your call centre and strap on a pair of headphones. It's as good a place as any to start understanding what your customers really think about your business, and what they *don't* want you to give them.

The Currency Of Courtesy

I remember once being 'courted' over lunch to get involved in a business deal. While it was a reasonable deal I was on the fence about getting involved, hence the lunch meeting. It started well, and I was beginning to buy into the vision they were presenting.

Then it went downhill. Fast.

The waiter brought the menus out, and the guy I was lunching with rudely told him to go away and come back in ten minutes. I remember pushing back in my chair thinking, "This just got interesting". During the rest of the lunch my associate continued being dismissive and rude towards the waiter.

The food was great. But I started losing my appetite for the deal.

The odd thing was that when he switched his attention back to me he was extremely charming and attentive—almost like Jekyll & Hyde. But I knew he was 'faking' it because he'd revealed his true self through his interactions with the waiter. Even though the deal was a good one (on paper) at the end of the lunch I politely declined my involvement. If he could treat a waiter just trying to do his job as poorly as he had, what would he be like with the pressures of leading a fast-growth business with limited time and resources? How would he build and manage a team when the pressure was on?

You can learn a lot about people from how they treat waiters in restaurants. But it may not all be good. In this case my lunch partner's behaviour cast doubts about his inter-personal skills, and how it could manifest itself in the pressures of building an early stage business.

It costs little to be courteous and respectful. The courtesy 'test' is repeated daily in how we behave in everyday circumstances, whether in a shop, a restaurant or a call centre. If you treat every interaction as a precious gift, even if it only lasts for a moment, you may learn something new and useful. Or you can demean the waiter, go home without a business deal done and wonder what happened.

The currency of courtesy should never be underestimated.

Great ideas and opportunities can come from the most unexpected places. And getting access to them might not take much more effort than being courteous and open-minded to the guy next to you in the coffee line, or the taxi driver taking you home.

Or the waiter serving you lunch.

But you'll never know if your prejudices get in the way of finding out. So be respectful, humble and inquisitive with everyone you meet no matter who they are, what they do or where they come from.

Every person does important work, and has a unique life with rich experiences and their own story to tell. And they're *all* interesting.

The key to unlocking those stories, ideas, imaginations and inspirations is to simply treat people the way you would like to be treated.

In other words, be human.

When 'I Don't Know' Is The Right Answer

In 2012 I was unexpectedly tapped on the shoulder by Meridian Energy Ltd to lead their efforts to launch their new Powershop brand into the Australian market. It was an intriguing offer, and after careful consideration I decided to get involved.

As part of the induction process I had to travel overseas because the Group CEO wanted to meet me, presumably to see if I had what it takes to put this new business on the ground. One of the first questions he asked was, "The market in Australia is homogeneous, undifferentiated and highly competitive. How do you intend to get customers in this environment?"

I answered truthfully that at that stage I didn't know, but in 3-4 months I'd have a much clearer view and some early customers on board.

"It's never easy to establish something new, especially with low brand awareness and, in this case, easily substitutable options for customers," I said. "To get to the right answers it's important not to try and jump too quickly to the end-game—it can be expensive and time consuming to do that. It's better to set up a disciplined regime of questioning, testing small 'moves' rapidly and learning as you go rather than being held to a more rigid game plan. It's also necessary to do it this way to allow time to build out and develop a new team into a cohesive unit.

"Key to this approach is asking lots of questions to discover the customers' current pain points and what might influence them to switch their patronage across. While I have some early views, without this information I'd just be guessing as to how we might get new customers on board."

After explaining this I remember pausing and saying, "So, no, I don't know where customers will come from. But I hope this explains how I intend to go about finding out".

He smiled and said, "Okay, fair enough" and then later, "Get on with it".

A couple of weeks later some feedback filtered back to me. He said it was refreshing that "someone told me the truth rather than trying to bluff me when they didn't have the answers".

I also remember when I met the Powershop team for the first time. I repeated what I had said to the Group CEO, namely that I didn't have all the answers (or, in fact, any), but I knew that as a team we'd figure it out together as long as we were prepared to experiment, take risks, work hard and always stayed focused on the needs of the customer.

The team took up the challenge and we were away.

In the end we got customers—lots of them—and figured out a replicable system to keep doing it. But it wasn't easy. Where we got them from was different in some ways to what we originally thought. But through the relentless circular method we adopted—trial, refine, discard/ proceed, refine, scale, etc.—we eventually unlocked the points of greatest customer dissatisfaction, and created an opportunity in the marketplace where we could focus our efforts with compelling and interesting product offers.

Along the way we learnt what did and didn't work. We didn't have pre-set notions, and weren't locked to a plan as to where customer acquisitions should come from, which helped up greatly. We were prepared to learn as we went and prove our conclusions based on real-world interactions with customers. In the end what mattered most was that results were delivered, not whether we knew the answers up front.

These days I still answer some questions with "I don't know" because it's the truth. But that only starts the discovery process. I now know that discipline, good process, creativity, nimbleness and hard work properly applied are the 'magic' that eventually uncovers the answers you don't know now but will uncover soon enough if you are prepared to do the hard work to find out.

The 80:20 Rule

Here is a little theory of mine. It isn't based on research, but rather 30 years of personal observation across many businesses.

The average person spends approximately 20-25% of their work time (one day a week) engaged in non-productive activities. This includes dealing with personal matters, office gossip and general procrastination that don't contribute value to an organisation.

But what if you could halve that number? Would it have a significant impact on your organisation? Unlocking the power of the 80/20 rule could help you do that.

The 80/20 rule, also known as Pareto's Principle, means that in any given situation a few things (20%) are critical and many (80%) are not. The actual percentages aren't that important—they could be 90/10 or 50/50. What's important is understanding that a few things will have a much greater impact than many others.

In simple terms, this could mean that 20% of any time and effort expended will produce 80% of your results. That's a sobering number. It could mean 80% of your sales will come from 20% of your sales team, customer base, distribution channels and pipeline opportunities. And from a team perspective, 20% of your staff will produce 80% of your HR headaches!

Imagine what would happen if you removed as much of the "bad" 80% as possible and used the available time and resources more productively.

Prioritisation is key to applying the 80/20 rule effectively. At the top level, management should determine the small number of matters that will have the greatest performance impact. That's the hard part. If you can't identify what they are, you won't be able to focus on them and discard or delegate the less important matters.

It reminds me of a company I coached a few years ago. It had a solid ten-year history selling products to a growing sector, and was well respected with a good market position. Twelve months before my involvement they decided to diversify their offering and grow their business by acquisition. They acquired a business that operated in an entirely different industry and once the transaction was complete they quickly merged the two businesses together.

It was a disaster from day one. The acquired business had rudimentary systems and processes, and a poor culture. It was heavily people-reliant, and the immediate loss of several key staff nearly forced its closure. Senior management spent months trying to mesh the two businesses together, but the differences made it impossible. The company started to bleed cash and nearly went under.

And that's where I entered the picture. I could see immediately that that the acquisition was a poor one. It didn't fit the company's profile or its future plans. Management had diverted more than 50% of their time to manage the business, even though it represented less than 10% of their sales and none of their profits. Even with a successful turnaround plan the business would never be big in the scheme of things. Worst still, the core business, which had always been profitable, was now losing money too and needed additional working capital to survive.

Left with no other viable option, I recommended the acquired business either be closed or sold quickly. A year before, the business had been acquired for a substantial sum. But now it was almost worthless with no prospects for recovery, and was forcing the overall company to the edge.

It was a bitter and expensive pill for the company directors to swallow. But they agreed, and the business was wound down. After this the company refocused on what it was good at, and slowly rebuilt the core business. Four years later it's in good shape and growing steadily.

The 80/20 rule is a useful reminder to focus most of your time on the small number of things that will create the most value. It's not a rigid rule, more a guiding principle to keep you focused and on track. The key is not just to work smart but also to work on the right things.

Half-delegating Is Dumb Business

Would you book a plane ticket on an airline you half-trusted? Or let a surgeon operate on you if he'd only completed half of the required clinical training? Or lend someone money if you rated your chances of getting it back no better than half?

No, obviously.

And that's why you shouldn't half-delegate to someone unless you're sure they can get the job done 100% on their own. Delegation is entirely about trust. And you have to trust the person fully before you delegate anything important to them.

There are two distinct parts to the delegation process:

- Delegating the work
- Delegating the responsibility

Effective delegation involves delegating the responsibility, not just the work. So if you only half-trust someone then you shouldn't delegate to them. Half-delegation requires constant dabbling in what's been delegated which creates frustration for everybody involved. Some executives like this approach (dabbling) but nobody else will.

By all means delegate the work if you're not sure they're yet ready or capable of doing the task. But don't give them the overall responsibility. Instead, mentor them closely until you're comfortable. While you're mentoring them, make it clear that you've delegated the work but not the responsibility. This process may take days, weeks or even months, so be patient. The most important thing is to give them the tools and experience they'll need to confidently take on the responsibility when they *are* ready.

When you've decided the time is right to *fully* delegate you need to ensure that you allow your team time and space to get on with the job without trying to micro-manage them.

In my own experience I have significantly changed how I manage people. When I was younger I was more concerned about the minutia of what they doing every day, how long they had for lunch, how many personal calls they made and whether they arrived on time or left early etc.

Over time, I learned a better way. I learned to manage outcomes, not style or behaviour. I now care less about how people do things and more about whether they are working on the right things and are being productive.

This profoundly changed my conversations with the teams I've been involved with. It forced me to establish (and agree) clear, unambiguous performance expectations up front. It wasn't simple to begin with but it eventually morphed into four simple principles that now guide the behaviours of all the teams I've managed in recent times:

1. The quality of the work must be high
2. Deadlines must be achieved
3. The reputation of the business cannot be damaged
4. Everyone must be a team player

I tell my team members - "I don't mind how, when or where you complete your work; that is up to you; what I care about is these four matters so adopt your own style and methods and be creative. If you need help I'll help you. You just have to ask. I won't micro-manage you but I expect you to live up to what we have agreed."

Done properly this approach can unlock the *discretionary efforts* of the team. Discretionary effort occurs when people *decide* to make the extra effort because they choose to, not because they are asked to. They do it because they understand their contribution is important, that the organisation values them individually and trusts them and consequently is prepared to provide them "room" to do their job in the way that suits them best.

It's a two-way commitment.

It also takes some of the emotion out of managing people because the expectations are clear and the conversation is focused on outcomes, not effort or style. The only proviso is you can't set them up to fail by not providing necessary coaching, mentoring and general assistance when required.

In an environment where outcomes count it's a much better approach than looking over someone's shoulder and reprimanding them for coming back from lunch 10 minutes late or worrying whether their last sick day was legitimate or was spent at the beach.

Sooner or later you'll need to delegate part or all of your work to someone else. It's inevitable. And there are benefits to delegating effectively. By creating a workforce of empowered managers and workers with clear parameters of operation who can be trusted to get the job done, the business will steam ahead.

You'll know when you're making strong progress when you are able to honestly say to your people - *use your best judgement at all times. I trust you to make good decisions and to get it done.*

Keep Your Presentations Short And Sharp

"I hate being presented to. Long-winded overhead presentations bore me to tears and I switch off when they're on. I don't need to hear all the underlying research that led to the conclusion being presented on the final slide. What I need to hear is your recommendation and why you think it's the best course of action for us. That's it. If I need to ask questions about the data or the supporting evidence I'll ask them. But if I don't then leave it out. I need the process to be efficient and meaningful. I don't want to waste time—yours or mine. So get to the point and make it snappy."

As close as I can remember that's how one of my biggest customers responded to a presentation I made to them a number of years ago. It was blunt and harsh criticism, but he was right. I treated his time as a luxury and not with the level of professional courtesy it deserved.

I'd fallen into the trap of believing customers (or anyone) would be impressed by long presentations showing how diligently I'd researched a subject and how flashy I could make my PowerPoint slides. I'd missed the point entirely. What impresses people most is the quality of the insights, not the length or dazzle of the presentation.

He called me on it. And I haven't done it since.

These days I rarely use PowerPoint presentations, and when I do I limit the number of slides. And they're never "data heavy"—I use them as prompts only, not to convey substantive information.

Thanks to the Internet, information that may have been difficult to obtain (even proprietary) in the past is now likely to be available in the public domain. It's available to everyone, and relatively easy to find. The real skill is taking large volumes of information from multiple sources, distilling it, and then using it to construct concise and logical arguments that are easy to understand and get to the point quickly, compellingly and unambiguously.

It's not easy to do, and I haven't seen too many people do it well. But if you can get there by using 500 words instead of 5,000 and five minutes instead of 50, you're well on your way.

A Simple Matrix To Spend Money Wisely

Sometimes it's a challenge knowing how and where to spend money sensibly. Money is easy to waste and there is only a finite supply of it so making it stretch as far as possible, while advancing towards your goals, is a critical success requirement.

Over the years I've used a simple matrix to determine what's sensible to spend money on. It works like a filter, and is based on a series of simple questions that start with this one: "Would our customers be prepared to pay for this?"

This refers to any issue at any level in an organisation. If you don't think your customers will pay for it then it probably won't create value. It's a (deliberately) tough question to ask.

If the answer is "Yes" then the action needs further scrutiny. I do this by applying the following criteria:

- **Essential.** Is it essential? That is, do we have to do it because we have no choice or because the economic upside (or downside) makes it too compelling not to?
- **Worth Considering.** Would it make our lives easier? Would it make us more efficient and/or improve our customers' experience with us if we implemented it?
- **Nice To Have.** Can we do without it? Is there a significant downside if we choose not to do it?

The quicker you can separate potential actions into "Essential" (must do these), "Worth Considering" (do the best ones) and "Nice To Have" (avoid if possible), the quicker you can start prioritising where to spend money sensibly.

The second requirement is to establish simple disciplines that will allow you to transparently review the quality of the decisions (regarding spending money) that are being made in your organisation.

One of the best disciplines is to sign every cheque, or electronic payment, personally. Scrutinising every payment will quickly alert you to things that just don't look quite right. It will also force your team to give more thought to what is being submitted, if they know you are reviewing it. This raises the level of accountability and minimises bad practices. You'll probably save money too.

The reason I like the *sign every cheque rule* is that it gives me regular, cheap, internal due diligence about my business without the need to be intimately involved in every initiative or activity. It gives me the opportunity to intervene and challenge decisions being taken recognising that I have ultimate responsibility for the company's financial health.

For fifteen years I signed every cheque in the businesses I managed or owned with staggering success. Even as the businesses got larger I continued to do it. I didn't like doing it, of course, as it was tedious and boring work. But it was important and I made the time to do it. The benefits far outweighed the aggravation. Admittedly, with the advent of electronic payments it's got simpler and easier.

Streamlining the process makes it less painful for everyone. I was available on Wednesday mornings each week to sign and approve payments. This provided a focal point for accounts and expense management and was well-known to both our staff and suppliers.

Most small and medium sized companies can benefit from the *sign every cheque* rule, even it is slightly expanded beyond one person (to a small handful) doing it. The point is that someone needs to be ultimately in control that has an understanding of the overall financial profile (and strategy) of the company and can make sensible 'spending' decisions based on using that knowledge.

Between the simple matrix described above and the *sign every cheque* rule it's an effective way to regulate and spend money. Give it a try. It's worked great for me.

The Magic Number To Unlock Value In Your Business

In the early days of Calendar Club I learned it didn't pay to have a large set of company-wide performance tracking numbers in your business. A small number of key performance indicators (KPIs) were critical, but too many would be counter-productive. The key for me was finding the magic number(s) in our business that would galvanise the efforts of the team and really drive performance.

We discovered that we would create the most value by focusing on increasing the number of multiple sales made (i.e. transactions comprising more than one item). Before focusing on it our multiple sales were less than 20% of all transactions. After two years of consistent effort we increased it to 30%, which lifted our absolute sales by 8%.

This was done without increasing the number of transactions or our cost base, or engaging in price discounting. This action, combined with our strong growth in store numbers each year, had a dramatic effect on our bottom line. We'd found our magic number.

But we had to do more than just measure it. We had to adjust our entire operations to extract the value we were after. So we aligned our total operational efforts behind answering one simple question: "If we [insert action being considered], will it help us increase multiple sales?" If it did, we implemented it. If it didn't, we moved on.

This simple approach was a strong contributing factor in our rapid rise to market leadership.

Another business that I coached a few years ago was struggling to get traction in its sector. It had an unclear market proposition and a confusing product offering. We spent time simplifying its business model, improving its offerings and determining its best sales channels. We then got to work on discovering the magic number(s) that would unlock the future value of the company.

In the end we concluded that each salesperson had to make sales pitches to 12 prospective clients each week and convert 20% of them to a sale. Their magic number became "12 x 20%" and they coordinated all their efforts to hitting those numbers. Within three months the company was achieving a level of sales activity previously thought unattainable.

Finding your magic number can be difficult sometimes. It may not be obvious, and will be different for every business. Do you know what yours is?

The Small Stuff Is Important.

When I was a kid, my father (an ex-army officer) used to patrol the house turning off any unnecessary lights as he went. He still does. Dad is a 'waste not, want not' type of guy. Spending your childhood in the tough years of the 1930s, with very limited means, teaches you to conserve resources and make the most of what you have. It's a good life skill.

This mindset has rubbed off on me, and it has guided how I operate in business. I unashamedly turn lights off and scour for opportunities to save money whenever I can. Waste is an enemy of business, and I root it out and remove it wherever it is.

My philosophy is simple—don't spend money unless it makes you more money. That means stripping out anything your customers wouldn't be prepared to pay for in higher prices. It gives you a razor-sharp focus and an honest approach to business that customers appreciate.

But this attitude is about more than just about turning lights off and saving money. It's about noticing and acting on anything that can be improved in your business. Loose electrical cords under a desk, old magazines in the reception area, telephones that aren't answered, debtor days creeping out, bins overflowing, slow order processing and customer parking spots occupied by staff vehicles are sure signs management is out to lunch.

Roger Corbett, ex-CEO of Woolworths, knew this all too well. Legend has it he once found a Woolworths shopping trolley in Sydney's Circular Quay, near the Opera House. He pushed it 1.5kms to return it to a store near the Town Hall wearing his "My name is Roger" name badge, which he wore everywhere.

Roger knew that if he set the best example on the small stuff, there was a good chance everyone would follow, creating an exponential effect on the company culture. The not-so-subtle message was, "If I'm prepared to do it, then you should be too".

It must have worked. During his seven years as CEO, the market capitalisation of Woolworths increased from $18.5bn to $37bn. Not bad for a bloke pushing a shopping trolley.

Don't delude yourself—this stuff matters. The small stuff is a window to the heart, soul and underlying health of any business. If small problems are left unattended the business will eventually soften up, service levels will deteriorate, the internal culture will suffer, and customers will get fed up and leave. It's a slippery slope from that point on.

The important thing is to get the balance right between the big picture activities and the smaller day-to-day ones. Fixing the small problems as soon as you find them will provide more time later to focus on more strategic matters when they emerge. The key is to fix them properly so they never need fixing again.

Next time you see a light on in an empty room, a bin that needs emptying or a phone that should be answered, don't look around for someone else to do it. Do it yourself. The practicalities of saving money, improving efficiency or satisfying a customer should be reason enough. But the symbolic value of acting quickly and decisively, regardless of your rank in the company, is priceless.

The Price Is Right

A few years ago I watched a TV interview with guy who'd just started a new business. He'd leased office space in the downtown precinct of an Australian capital city for $330 per square metre and was delighted because the "market price was closer to $500 per square metre".

Intrigued, I dug around (i.e. did a Google search), located the building he was in, and quickly learned there was still office space available for lease. I rang the leasing agent and, without negotiating, was offered space for $340 per square metre in the space of five minutes.

So much for *that* market price.

Correctly pricing a company's goods and services is one of the most fundamental tasks of an organisation, especially in today's hyper-competitive global economy.

Getting it right is critical. It requires a deep understanding of the marketplace, how it's evolving, what customers consider valuable and, most importantly, what they're prepared to pay for.

Many businesses use a simple cost-plus methodology to set their prices. They calculate their input costs (product and/or service costs) add a margin, and the result is the price they charge. And, every year or so they expect to put their prices up without doing anything different.

Unfortunately this ignores the competitive dynamics of a marketplace, and is especially concerning in a market that's relatively homogenous, competitive, evolving quickly or where switching costs are low.

The essence of price setting is getting the balance right between the forces of supply (you) and demand (your customers). Put simply, it's determining the price point where you make 'enough' money to make it financially worthwhile for you versus the 'traction' point where enough customers are prepared to buy because they think it's valuable at that price. And the intersection, where both sides are happy, is arguably where the most money gets made.

But this only goes part of the way, and you need to do more than this to protect yourself. You need to be able to sell at a price below where most customers (existing and potential) would buy anyway—below the intersection point described earlier—and still make a satisfactory financial return.

Why? Because you can no longer expect to pass annual price increases on to your customers without losing business. You have to do more than that because smart customers will have contingency plans in place so they can walk away. If you're relying on annual price increases to sustain yourself, it might be time for a re-think.

This doesn't mean you have to cut prices, and I am not suggesting you should. What I *am* saying is you should have the capacity to cut them if you ever need to (or even want to). Being able to do so will offer some protection from unfavourable macro-events and price wars, and give you opportunities when your competitors are vulnerable. Think of it an insurance policy you may never have to use.

This means operating a lean cost structure where waste and fat is cut away. You need an extremely efficient, truncated supply chain where every dollar spent makes a return. In the end what you're trying to do is get your product or service into your customers' hands by the most direct and cost-effective method possible.

The ultimate prize is a product or service that customers love and want and with a market price that's attractive for everyone. But there's nothing wrong with taking out some 'insurance' to protect yourself in case the market price starts to slide or your competitors get into trouble.

In the meantime get lean, smile, and enjoy the extra margins.

Getting Paid On Time

One of my pet hates is when customers don't pay their bills on time. It's even worse when clear payment expectations are agreed up-front, the goods or services are delivered, and then no payment is received. All that follows is excuses.

It's a quick way to erode trust.

Too many businesses, desperate to win a client, will gloss over how and when they expect to get paid. They'll just cross their fingers and hope they're dealing with someone they can trust. In the end they have to deal with a problem they could have avoided if they were clearer and more up-front with their expectations.

A company I know suffered from weak cash flow due to a long-dated debtor book. Their sales were growing strongly every year, but they had weak credit controls that needed fixing quickly. They came up with an approach that was straightforward and honest, which they communicated to their clients. With their permission I've reproduced this excerpt:

"We try to keep our prices as low as possible at all times. We are not a bank so this only works if we are paid on time. Our standard payment terms are 14 days from invoice. If you would like to pay cash up front then we will reduce the price by 2.5%. If you would prefer to pay in 30 days that is fine too but your price will be increased by 2.5%. We don't offer terms any longer than that.

You can choose which of these payment terms suit you best.

To stress how important it is for us to be paid on time we will call you the day after a payment is due if you haven't paid it. We will request immediate payment and remind you what we agreed today. We would prefer to be up-front about this to avoid any hard feelings later on.

We assume this is all acceptable but we're happy to talk through any specific matters you might have. We are very excited to be working with you and can't wait to get started."

I recently spoke to the business owner, and he told me sales, cash flow and customer satisfaction had improved significantly. It took a few months to clean up his debtor book, and they had to shed some clients along the way who refused to pay on time. But in his words, "We're better off working with companies that live up to their promises".

And he's absolutely right.

Brainstorm With Discipline

I love a good brainstorming session. Throw a diverse group of people together with different experiences and backgrounds, give them a problem to solve, add some time pressure and you've got a good formula for getting something done.

You will, however, need to agree a brainstorming approach to ensure you get the most out of your efforts. Should it be a free-for-all democratic process where everyone's voice and opinion is considered carefully and equally? Should it be a brain dump of ideas that quickly get filtered down to a few worth exploring further? Or should it be something else entirely?

In my own experience I've struggled with the free-for-all approach. It sounds great in principle, but it can get bogged down because everyone tries to be nice and democratic about everyone else's ideas. The truth is some ideas are good and some aren't, and sooner or later you need to cut through them to get to the good ones.

To achieve cut-through in any brainstorming session, a strong set of rules needs to be agreed up-front. Here are some that I use:

- Start by precisely framing and understanding the problem you're trying to solve. This is the most difficult part, and the one people typically spend the least time on. But unless you really understand the problem you can't move to the solution stage.

- Focus on these three questions:
  - Is the problem worth solving and why?
  - What are the options to solve it?
  - Which is the best option and why?

- Start with an 'anything is possible' approach. The focus should be on creation and innovation, not hanging on to the past or limiting the possibilities.
- Get a diverse group together—all levels and departments plus some outsiders, if possible — and let every idea be heard, even the wild ones. Move through them all quickly until you get to the bigger, more substantive ones that will most likely solve the problem.
- Appoint a strong facilitator to guide the session, keep it on track and make sure it's moving forward.
- Ensure there's only one conversation at a time, and give everyone a reasonable amount of time to air their views. But stay focused on solving the problem.
- Don't worry about how you'll execute the solution(s). That comes later.
- Keep it short – smash it in 60-90 minutes.

The biggest benefit of a great brainstorming session is drawing on the organisation's wider collective intelligence, and applying that intellect in a structured manner to address a problem that needs to be solved.

At its core, brainstorming is all about collaboration, instinct and innovation. One person may start things off, but it's everyone else's obligation to build on that, take it further, push the envelope and ultimately take it to a new place. Done well, it creates a powerful chain reaction of energised collaboration and creativity that produces something new and wonderful.

All you need to get started is a whiteboard, some Post-it notes, an absence of hierarchy and an hour or so of time. Plus some open, diverse minds, of course!

The Wisdom Of Old Dudes

I'm always slightly amused by how much emphasis gets put on youth in business. People over 50 are considered over the hill, and are being replaced by the new 'young guns' who are often still wet behind the ears.

Why is this? Do we really believe the cumulative life and business experience of a 50-, 60- or even 80-year-old is less valuable than a kid who can build an app?

I remember during the tech wreck of the 1990s how one stock market analyst said there was a "new paradigm" about valuing Internet stocks. Apparently you couldn't value them like 'old economy' stocks. It wasn't about earnings, assets and debt levels any more. It was about "how the world will change" as a result of the new technologies. This analyst was in her late twenties and relatively inexperienced. But she was a convincing speaker, which helped her deliver her sermon to a wide audience.

The problem was she was making it up as she went along, but the punters wanted to believe her (and did). She wasn't the only one of course. Spruiking like this led to inflated Internet stock prices and an eventual fall in the Nasdaq index of nearly 75%. Even ten years later in 2010 the Nasdaq was still trading at only 50% of its high point in 2000. Billions were lost. How was this possible?

Warren Buffet, nearly 70 at the time, called it "irrational exuberance" and didn't participate. He warned that the huge returns experienced by technology investors during 1998 and 1999 had made them complacent. "After a heady experience of that kind," he said, "normally sensible people drift into behaviour akin to that of Cinderella at the ball. They know that overstaying the festivities will eventually bring on pumpkins and mice."

A lifetime of experience had taught him it was a bubble that would soon burst. He was criticised for being out of touch, but he was right and the punters were wrong. Only years at the coalface teaches you these types of lessons.

After 30 years in business I still regularly seek the advice and counsel of people more experienced than me. I've learnt a lot with this approach, and avoided mistakes I otherwise would have made. My formula (which I half-jokingly call my "virtuous circle of decision making") goes like this.

I figure out the "why" (the motive) myself. I ask my mentors for help with moulding the "what" (the objective), and get answers from more technically adept people to help with the "how" (how to put it on the ground).

It works great for me.

History has a way of repeating itself. The 'old-timers' have seen multiple boom and bust economic cycles, and the fashion, movies, music and other trends from the 50s, 60s, 70s, 80s and 90s being recycled for a contemporary audience. They have an encyclopaedia of life and commercial experience that can be invaluable to businesses of all sizes.

The axiom that you can't put an old head on young shoulders is sage advice. So why not tap into the wisdom and skills that suitably qualified "grey-hairs" can provide? The downside is limited but the upside might be just the advantage you need.

Networking 24/7

As the saying goes, "It's not what you know, it's who you know". And thanks to the Internet we can connect with more people than ever before.

But while finding people may be easier, making that connection can be difficult. You need to find the right people at the right time and for the right reasons.

Most importantly, you should be looking for more than just help or advice. You should be looking to make a connection that benefits both parties.

Keep making connections even when you don't need to

It's easy to get caught up in the grind of the nine-to-five. Catch the same train to work every day. Sit in the same seat. Have coffee at the same time. Buy your sandwich at the same place. Read the same newspaper. Deal with the same customers, suppliers and advisors. Talk to the same people about the same things. And expect that nothing will ever change.

It's comfortable, predictable and familiar. And it works fine—until something unexpected happens.

A guy I know fell into this trap. He was cruising along nicely until the 2008 GFC hit and he unexpectedly lost his job. Many of his colleagues met a similar fate. Cast adrift, he realised his contact base was small and the industry he operated in had shrunk to half its former size.

Stuck with a large mortgage and high living expenses, he started calling recruiters, sent out hundreds of Linked-in invitations, and contacted old colleagues he hadn't spoken to in years. This went on until he finally got a job a year later.

It was tough to watch.

In hindsight he admitted he should have been more proactive when things were going well. With the share market roaring along for most of the decade he'd convinced himself the party would continue forever. He got lazy. He made no effort to make new connections, expand his sphere of influence or learn new skills. He was blinded by the money he was making, and couldn't (or wouldn't) see the cliff approaching.

He was playing a short game when you needed to play long.

The same applies for businesses. It's easy to show up, do your thing every day and go home. It's a nice life until it ends.

And it always ends.

I've learnt that lesson the hard way. Subsequently, whenever I get involved in a new business I make it a rule to meet two new people every week for the first three to four months. That's 25 new people. And I'd have lunch, or at the very least coffee, with one of them every week.

That's a lot of people. And it's hard to maintain, especially when things heat up. But the effort is worth it. Even now when things slow down for me I go back to this rule. Within three or four weeks the momentum starts to build and I'm off and running again.

But it's naïve to think your fortunes will improve just by meeting a bunch of new people. That's rarely the case. The people you meet are busy too, and you can't expect them to solve your problems or automatically invite you into their 'successful' world. You have to earn that right.

You do that by helping them too. Introduce them to a colleague or acquaintance they might find interesting, alert them to something happening in the market they didn't know about, or assist them in some other way. Don't expect anything back. Relationships take time to build, and the good people in business will remember your help when an opportunity that suits you comes their way. It might take months, years or even a decade or two, so it's important to constantly expand, refresh and work on your contact base.

Don't be disappointed if some connections don't develop or stick. Some people won't be a good match, and some aren't worth worrying about. Others might be a slow burn. Just be nice, genuine, interested and engaged in the relationships you form. People are more likely to help and do business with people they like.

Like anything worthwhile, building deep, valuable and enduring connections takes time and effort. It's important to nurture them and develop them, so don't take them for granted. The great ones are like old friends—hard to find and difficult to replace.

How To Meet Anyone

"Hi mate. Just thought I'd reach out to you. You seem to be doing some interesting things and I'd love to buy you a coffee sometime and chat."

I got this Linked In message from someone I didn't know. He wasn't referred to me, and didn't provide any details about who he was, what he wanted to talk about, and why that might be interesting to me. Basically it was a lazy cold call. Chat and coffee with a stranger for an undefined purpose? No thanks.

Compare this to the approach I got from another person (abridged version):

"Hi Paul. A mutual colleague 'Joe Smith' speaks highly of you and suggested that I make contact to discuss a potential business synergy that we both think might be valuable to you. As an aside I have been an avid reader of your blog and I have followed your work for quite some time. I know that you are really busy and I don't want to waste your time but if you can spare me 10 minutes to talk through my idea I would be really grateful. John."

I called him and we ended up doing business together. Why? Because he did some homework, got a strong referral, was respectful, had something to offer me and promised not to waste my time. It's an irresistible combination, no matter how busy you are.

One of the best stories I've ever heard was at a conference from a successful entrepreneur describing his start-up days in the early 1990s. He desperately needed to meet an investor he believed could provide much-needed capital and expertise to his fledging enterprise. The problem was the investor was extremely busy and seemingly unreachable.

Not sure how to get the investor's attention, he chose to write a letter detailing the warts-and-all journey of his venture so far and how much he could benefit from ten minutes of the investor's time.

He got no response.

Undeterred, he wrote eight more letters—one each week—and hand-delivered each one. He never got past the receptionist's desk. He changed tactics and took to calling the investor every week while continuing to write weekly letters describing his latest progress.

For three months he got no response. Finally the investor called him and asked bluntly, "What do I have to do to get rid of you"?

The entrepreneur responded with, "Give me ten minutes of your time."

"Okay. Be at my office at 8am tomorrow and don't be late."

The ten-minute meeting led to a relationship that endured for several years. Sometimes extreme circumstances call for extreme measures.

Successful people are always busy and have limited time available for coffee, lunch or other niceties. In a perfect world they'd respond to every request they got. But that's impossible, so only the interesting ones will get their attention.

That interest gets created if the other person believes there's a good reason to meet. And your job is to demonstrate that to them. Getting a referral from a trusted source doesn't hurt either.

And when you finally *do* meet them face-to-face, always be respectful, empathetic, positive and enthusiastic.

Tips From The Best Networker I Know

I have a friend called "Phil". He's a quiet, unassuming guy known by a wide cross-section of people. He's also a 'go-to-guy', and the best networker I have ever met.

One time he let me in on his secret, which I now call 'extreme networking'. And it's amazing to watch in action.

Whenever Phil gets invited to any business event (or any event for that matter) he always asks the host who else is attending. Whenever possible, he asks for the guest list. He's expert at obtaining it. For small events, such as a round table lunch session for ten people, he insists on getting at least the names and email addresses of every participant in advance.

He then researches who'll be attending the function. He wants to know as much about each person as he possibly can before he arrives at the event. He checks them out online and asks his contacts about them if he can. He has a naturally personable approach, and people are happy to help him out. He returns the favour whenever possible, and is very discreet.

What sets Phil apart is his preparation. He has a great 30-second personal elevator pitch that's compelling, humorous and low-key. It took him more than a year to perfect it. It's authentic, and people immediately connect with him as a result.

Because he prepares in advance, people are delighted he knows something about them and their business. He asks intelligent, insightful questions, which makes him memorable. He makes it look natural, but he's done his homework.

While most people are bumbling around explaining what they do to the person next to them, Phil is creating bonds. He's made a deeper connection, and people feel special and valued as a result. He's a very genuine guy, which becomes obvious when you meet him.

He doesn't talk about himself, and doesn't try to sell anything. He's easy to trust because he's totally focused on the other person.

He's also expert at working the room, rarely getting caught in boring, unproductive conversations. He's there to work and he takes his job seriously. His approach works, and I've lost track of how many people have told me what a great guy he is.

When an event is over Phil always sends everybody he met a personalised email saying how much he enjoyed their company and congratulating them on their business achievements. He keeps in touch too, and makes an effort to put together people in his network who, in his words, "should meet each other". He gets a kick out of doing this.

His network of adoring fans is huge.

Phil is a successful guy. Modestly, he once told me he's been successful not because he's one of the smartest guy around (in his words, he's not) but because he's one of the hardest workers. His mantra is, "if I can't out-think them then I'll out-work them". He applies this ethos of discipline, preparation and diligence to his networking efforts.

I once told him I thought he was a phenomenal networker. He laughed and told me he just loves meeting new people and helping them out whenever he can. He doesn't consider it networking.

He's right. It's extreme networking. And Phil's the best at it that I've ever seen.

Negotiating IOI

Negotiating is as much an art as a skill, and you'll only get better by doing it over and over.

But no matter how experienced you are, it always pays to follow a few guidelines.

Become an Expert Negotiator

Successful negotiations are about being prepared, confident, calm and humane. Whatever's being negotiated, it must be something the other person wants. There's no point negotiating if the other party doesn't actually want it, or if their position is so far removed from yours a negotiated outcome is unlikely.

Here's a list of negotiating strategies I have used successfully over many years and hundreds of negotiations:

- Be prepared. Don't underestimate the need to plan and prepare. Know the subject matter. Anticipate responses from the other person, and plan how to deal with them. Bad negotiators are usually ill-prepared, and suffer as a result.
- Not negotiable. Determine in advance what you need and want from the negotiation, including what's negotiable and what isn't. This defines your walk away position, and knowing it in advance relieves the pressure and allows for a less emotional negotiation. It also reduces the effectiveness of any intimidation tactics the other party might use. The key is knowing what you want and what you'll give away to conclude the negotiation.
- Listen more. Active listening is the key to solving most negotiating problems. It involves recognising both the verbal and non-verbal cues that can highlight what's most important to the other person. Understanding these cues can allow the discussion to move more easily to a negotiated outcome.
- Talk less. The philosophy of keeping your cards close to your chest is a good one. Provide information and arguments that only advance the

negotiation. Limit any dialogue to this. Talking too much may give the other party information they can use against you during the negotiation.

- Smart is dumb. Socrates used the principle of 'smart is dumb' by feigning ignorance to encourage others to express their views more fully. Today, many successful people have perfected the art of 'smart is dumb' by active listening, asking for things to be explained several times, and asking lots of questions.

- No rush. Make sure there's enough time for the negotiation. Take your watch off and don't look at the clock. If the meeting takes an hour or a week, make sure you're available for the entire time. If another meeting is needed, make sure it's the other party who asks for it. Make it clear you are here to finalise the matter now.

- Good body language. Smile. Nod a lot. Uncross your arms. Lean Forward. Consider sitting next to the person instead of across the table from them. Take notes. Give 100% attention. Maintain eye contact. Phones off. Be patient.

- Good verbal language. Speak at a consistent volume and speed. Pause for effect. Use silence when you need to. Ask thoughtful open-ended questions. Be empathetic. Graciously concede a point when you need to.

- No-one's right. Most people have different perspectives, even on the same issue. There's no point in trying to force your views onto the other person. It's not personal, so be gracious, even if you don't agree with the other person. Spend your time understanding the other person's perspective, and craft a solution that lets both of you come away with a win.

- Who's the decision maker? There's no point in negotiating with someone who doesn't have the ultimate authority to make a deal. Ask in advance whether the person has the authority to conclude the deal without having to refer it upwards.
- Don't negotiate with yourself. If you put forward a proposal and the other party responds with 'you're going to have to do better than that' or 'is this negotiable?' ask them for their counter-proposal. Don't offer up a counter-proposal yourself. Make them work for a better deal.
- When it's done, it's done. Shake hands. Put the agreement in writing quickly. Sign it. Move on. If you don't do it quickly, the other party could potentially change their mind or want to change something already agreed. Speed in execution will minimise this possibility.

Business is a long game, and one successful negotiation is just that—*one* successful negotiation. Whatever the outcome, you'll wake up tomorrow and have to deal with the same people again and again—customers, suppliers, partners and staff.

J. Paul Getty summed it up best: "My father said, 'You must never try to make all the money that's in a deal. Let the other fellow make some money too, because if you have a reputation for always making all the money, you won't have many deals'."

The Best Negotiating Lesson I Ever Learnt

A few years ago I was involved in negotiating a deal that could propel a company into the big league. Negotiations were progressing well until a stalemate was reached and neither party could see a way through. Despite many attempts they couldn't reach a compromise, and there was a good chance that the deal would fall through. Then it started to get nasty, with both sides accusing each other of sabotaging the deal.

At this point we surmised that continuing to negotiate would be counter-productive, and we chose to walk away.

We didn't make the decision lightly. The deal was important to us, and would certainly have accelerated our growth plans. But we didn't have to do the deal. And the other side knew it. They also knew that once we walked away we weren't coming back any time soon. It rattled them, and forced them to make deep concessions.

Three months later we concluded the deal on more favourable terms than we previously thought possible.

We learnt an important lesson during that process— sometimes the only way to get the deal you want is to walk away from the table without it. But you have to mean it, and be comfortable with the consequences.

More importantly, the other side has to believe you mean it too. If they need to do the deal, and you've walked away, they'll have no option but to sweeten it for you. A deal rarely gets worse if you wait it out.

Of course, the success of this approach is diluted if the deal isn't important to the other party, or can be easily substituted with another option. But if this case it's unlikely to conclude on favourable terms (to you) anyway.

Sometimes you might find yourself in a situation where the best thing to do is walk away from a negotiation without a deal. Do it. It might seem counter-intuitive at the time, but in the right circumstances, it may be the only way to *eventually* get the deal you want.

Stop Typing And Do It In Person

If you need to get anything important done, do it in person.

Doing it face-to-face changes everything. It speeds things up, forces action and decisions, and moves critical matters forward more efficiently. It also adds a human element where you can leave your personal imprint (hopefully a good one) on the other person.

Unfortunately the proliferation of emails, text messages, Facebook posts and tweets means many people try to settle or deal with critical matters using non-face-to-face means.

It's especially true for emails. Don't get me wrong— email is fine for passing on information or for less important matters. But when things really count it just doesn't work. How can you have an effective negotiation by email? Or deal with a problematic staff issue? Or close a major sale? Or get a key relationship back on track? There's only one way—by actually speaking to the other person.

The problem with emails is it's difficult to write a great one. One that covers the key information in an easy-to-digest and logical way, with the right level of emotion and emphasis to get your point across while still recognising the needs of the other party. Too many emails are written with a one-sided view, which often results in a choice of words and tone that's aggressive, inflammatory, or at best ill-considered. Even if this wasn't the intent, it creates a fertile environment for confusion and misinterpretation that's never helpful.

That's why it's best to do any substantive business face-to-face. You may occasionally have to do it by phone, but only if there is no immediate option for a face-to-face meeting. Email should only be used to record conversations that have taken place, share information, or communicate simple, mechanical business matters.

For me it's an efficiency measure more than anything. I know I can get a lot more done in a 30-minute meeting than by any other means. Experience has taught me too that people are more reluctant to say 'no' in person.

I also know most people would rather deal with a real live human being than respond to words on a screen.

Selling It

Selling is one of those skills everyone has, even if they don't realise it. And it's a skill they need to have, because everyone in an organisation needs to 'sell it', regardless of whether they have the word 'Sales' in their job title.

Serve The Customer Or Serve Someone Who Does

These days I believe there are only two jobs in any organisation:

- those that serve the customer
- those that serve someone who does.

If your job doesn't do either of these, I'd question whether you're doing useful work.

I also question whether the days of the 'head office' or 'headquarters' should be over. The real action happens at the emotional point of contact with the customer, whether it's face-to-face, at a call centre or via an online chat or forum.

And that's where modern organisations need to centre themselves.

A traditional organisational hierarchy, where the CEO sits firmly at the top directing traffic from the corner office, has little chance of doing this effectively. The pyramid needs to be inverted, putting customers at the top and the CEO at the bottom. Symbolically, this means the CEO is the ultimate master-servant of the business, not servant-master.

Divide all the roles in your organisation into those who serve the customer and those who serve someone who does. Was there any roles left over? If there was, these need close scrutiny and some may need to be redesigned or even jettisoned.

You'll know you're making progress as a customer-centric organisation when everyone has the phone numbers of all the company's frontline staff on their speed dial.

Can You Sell?

"Can you sell?"

It's one of the first questions I ask when I'm looking to hire someone. And it doesn't matter what the role is either.

The reactions I've received from this simple question, ranging from pure horror to disdain to fear to amusement to "Of course I can", have always been instructive and interesting.

One guy who worked in strategy had a typical reaction. He initially thought he'd misheard the question, so I repeated it. Then he went quiet and started to look very confused until he said (in a very quiet voice) "You understand I work in strategy?"

"Yep, I sure do. So, can you sell or not?"

I ask this question to get a reaction. I want to see if the person understands that the obligation to 'sell the organisation' is a core responsibility of everyone who works there. I want to see whether they're willing and able to talk about, promote and ultimately sell the benefits of the business to others, even if it isn't a defined responsibility of their role.

It bemuses me that some marketers, strategists, finance people, administrators, creatives and even CEOs I know believe they have no obligation to sell anything. They believe the responsibility for sales and business development resides exclusively with those people who have the word 'sales' in their job titles. Even worse, many of them consider sales to be beneath them, as if talking to customers (existing and prospective) is less important than the next meeting they have to attend.

Here are a few things that I'm sure about after 30 years in business:

- Sales is the lifeblood of an organisation
- Most businesses fail because of a lack of revenue
- The ability to positively influence others—a key aspect of leadership—is learnt best by negotiating and selling (something)

Anybody can sell. It's a mindset more than anything else—a willingness to be continuously opportunity focused, and understanding every interaction you have is a chance to leave a positive impression. It takes practice of course, but the effort is well worth it. And it will protect you in the long term as well too.

But you have to want to do it, and that's the hard part.

So, can *you* sell?

The Three Customer Groups That Matter

A while ago a company I was involved with commissioned some external consultants to help us understand our customers better. These guys were specialists in their field, and they were very impressive. The work they produced was of a high standard, and satisfied the mutually agreed scope of works.

Unfortunately, the output only scratched the surface and didn't tell us anything we didn't already know. We needed deeper knowledge. But it was our fault, not theirs. We'd simply scoped the project wrong.

Disappointed, we decided to get back to basics to determine what we already knew about our customers and what we needed to know. Scratching our heads, we concluded there were only three groups that mattered to us:

- Our current customers—those who buy from us now
- Our past customers— those who used to buy from us but don't anymore
- Our non-customers—those who have never bought from us.

This simplified matters for us.

We started by analysing our best and most important customers first. We asked them what they liked about us, what kept them coming back, what we could do better to satisfy them and whether we had 100% of their business. It was very illuminating, and we learnt a couple of very important things we didn't know before.

We then dug deeper into our customer list and asked a sample of our middle- and lower-tier customers the same questions. This is where it started getting interesting. A lot of this sample group were very open in giving us an assessment of how we compared to our competitors. Interestingly, two relatively small issues were major problems for this group. This was a complete surprise to us, and we made it a priority to fix them.

We applied the same approach to our past customers. Using a combination of telephone and online methods, we asked a sample of them why they'd left us and what we could we change to get their business back. The same two issues our existing customers highlighted were the main reasons why more than 50% of them had left us. Once we fixed these problems, we started winning some of them back.

One thing we learnt during this process was that we spent a disproportionate amount of time on acquiring new customers instead of improving our offer and maximising our potential with our existing customers.

We also decided to spend time winning back our past customers, especially those who'd left us for reasons that no longer existed. By changing this around, and making sure we delivered on our 'updated' customer promise, we were eventually rewarded with a pleasant surprise—new business referred to us by our existing customers!

One area where businesses fall down is putting unnecessary impediments or obstacles in the way of customers – either when they are choosing to buy or during the buying process itself. Sometimes they don't even know they are doing it.

I've been (obliviously) guilty of it at times. It's easy to do to and requires vigilance to avoid.

It reminds me of my experience at one of Melbourne's best and most famous Italian restaurants a few years ago. Twelve of us had just enjoyed an incredible meal and a fantastic experience. It was a night to remember.

Until the $1,200 bill arrived.

$400 cash was produced with four credit cards to cover the balance. These were handed to the waiter who politely replied – "we don't split bills." We all looked at each other slightly bemused. We explained the circumstances to him but he just repeated the restaurant's policy. We asked to see the manager. Same thing happened – "we don't split bills."

Left to ponder our predicament we each decided to pay with cash. We all trudged to the nearest ATM (100 metres away), withdrew the cash and returned to the restaurant. It took 15 minutes.

Not impressed.

No tip was left and we pledged not to return.

*We don't split bill*s is a dumb rule, made in a vacuum, without considering the impact on customers. So what if you have to do a few extra credit card transactions? Isn't it better to have your customers raving about their night at your restaurant instead of recounting their trip to the ATM?

They'd understand that if they actually spent time walking in their customers shoes.

If you ever find yourself second-guessing your customers and making assumptions about what *you* think they're thinking and what's important to them, there's a good chance you might be wrong.

It's relatively easy to find out—just observe them or ask them.

The Interaction Is Just As Important As The Transaction

One of the least enjoyable customer service experiences I've ever had was more than a decade ago when I was a member of a gym chain. It was easy enough to sign up, and I was told if I needed to cancel the membership at any time all I'd need to do is provide one month's notice, no questions asked.

But in practice this wasn't true, in fact, cancelling my membership (which I needed to do after two years) was a nightmare.

Firstly, I couldn't cancel over the phone or even via email or written letter. I had to make an appointment with the gym manager. This was inconvenient, and made worse by the fact the manager had limited availability to meet. Frustrated, I asked why I needed to come in and why this simple matter couldn't be handled over the phone or via email. They said paperwork needed to be completed, and that the manager needed to "interview" me.

A meeting was finally scheduled two weeks later, and it quickly became apparent it was just a last ditch hard sell to convince me to stay.

Really, who needs a meeting to leave a gym?

Even worse, the monthly direct debit from my bank account continued after I'd left, and the hassle of rectifying it was something I'd rather forget. This company took the whole idea of "easy in, impossible out" to a whole new level.

Years later the company began floundering, and I heard that during their desperate fight for survival the executive team were once asked the simple question, "How many customers do you have?" Silence followed. The question was repeated. Finally one of their team piped up with: "We don't call them customers. We call them units."

When I heard this, it explained my experience with the company. I was a "unit", and that's how I felt. I didn't feel like a customer, person or anything resembling a human being. I was a statistic, and one they wanted to avoid appearing on their customer churn report—even if it meant deceiving me and wasting my time.

What I *do* know is great customer experiences come from organisations focusing on the interaction, not just the transaction. It includes every single touch point with a customer—even when they decide to leave. It seems obvious, but customers aren't units, transactions, seats, load or any other dumb term used to describe them behind closed doors.

So stop calling them that and treating them like that.

It Helps If They Like You

Don't underestimate the power of being liked by your customers. It may be the one thing that separates you from your competition.

Consider this not-so-uncommon example. You're really good at what you do. You have a lot of expertise, and you love your work. Once you win business, people stay with you because you provide a great service and deliver what your promise. But business is slow, and you're struggling to win new customers. Your sales pipeline is shallow, and you're unsuccessful in most of your sales pitches.

Your competitors, on the other hand, seem to be flourishing. They don't seem to be any better than you, but they're definitely *doing* a lot better than you. Scratching your head, you search for answers. What you find astounds you. People don't actually *like* you. They certainly recognise your expertise, but prefer to deal with someone else if possible.

And it's marginalised your business.

In his book, *The Likeability Factor: How to Boost Your L-Factor and Achieve your Life's Dreams*, Tim Sanders states that, "Life is a series of popularity contests". If you're credible, likeable and good at what you do, you'll win a lot more business than if you're not likeable.

Some of us were lucky enough to be born likeable and never had to work too hard at it. But many of us weren't, and had to work to constantly develop these traits. Rightly or wrongly, people viewed as likeable are considered honest, positive, humorous, polite, respectful and authentic. Conversely, unlikeable people are considered dishonest, negative, boring, rude, disrespectful and phony.

Being likeable isn't about creating a false persona. You must be genuine and authentic, and be able to deliver. It's an extremely powerful combination, and in some circumstances may be enough to separate yourself from your more powerful competitors and allow you to win business that you otherwise may not have.

I Hate Being 'Sold' To

One time I took a call from 'Richard', a self-professed logistics expert claiming he could definitely save one of the businesses I'm involved with tens of thousands of dollars in annual freight costs. He got to this assertion within the first 30 seconds of our phone conversation.

The problem was I didn't know Richard, and he'd never set foot inside our business. So I asked him how much our annual logistics cost was. He didn't know. Then I asked whether he could *guarantee* the dollar savings he quoted before we wasted any more time on this call. He blustered and crowed, and ended up pleading for a ten-minute meeting with me. I gave him my email address and told him we could meet if he sent me a note guaranteeing the saving.

I hate being 'sold' to, and I can spot a phony a mile off. Like most people, I'm happy to buy what I want without the need to be convinced or pitched to. All that's needed is for sales people to keep asking questions to uncover my underlying need, and then provide relevant information to help with the purchase decision. The good ones understand this, and do it. The great ones go one step further and introduce subtle emotional calls to action (urgency, special offers, etc.) as they're giving me the information I ask for.

The worst sales people do the opposite. They don't listen. They don't ask questions. They feign interest in helping you. They come pre-armed with their 'pitch', and try to deliver it whether you want to hear it or not. It's an impersonal, formulaic, archaic method that doesn't work.

What gets forgotten in this approach is your customers don't really care how *you* feel or what *you* want to achieve. Why would they? All they care about is how you make *them* feel, and whether they can trust you to help them achieve what they need. Treat them like a number and you'll piss them off. But come armed with an attitude that genuinely says "I'm here to try and improve your day" and you're off to a flying start.

If every interaction you have with a customer, or potential customer, leaves them feeling slightly happier, less stressed, more confident or more in control, that's enough. Business is a long game, and it's better to aim for small incremental improvements for your customers every time you interact than go for one big 'bang' you have no hope of repeating.

And if a logistics 'expert' named Richard ever cold-calls you, let him know I'm still waiting patiently for his email.

One Of The Most Important Words In Sales

A colleague of mine once complained it was taking him too long to convert prospects into customers. He sold a good service, had a recognisable and valuable point of difference in the market, and a generally happy group of existing customers. The problem was his sales growth and rate of new customer acquisition was poor. He couldn't understand why. He asked me for my view.

After digging around for a while it became clear his pipeline of prospects was too thin and he was spending too much time trying to convert too few prospects. A small list of prospects was being harassed too regularly, creating frustration both within the company and the prospects list. Instead of broadening the sales funnel, the business was too focused on trying to convert existing prospects who weren't ready to buy.

The business had forgotten one of the most important words in sales: "Next".

The philosophy of 'next' is you spend only the minimum amount of time on every prospect to determine whether or not they're likely to buy, and in what timeframe. This will vary on a case-by-case basis. If they want to buy now, spend time to sell to them. If they need more time, follow up later on a mutually agreed date. And if they don't want to buy at all, quickly move on to the next prospect.

It's important not to get too emotional about rejection. It's not personal. Sales is a numbers game, and you can't force anyone to buy from you. What is important is the size of the sales funnel and the work being put into expanding it.

The best businesses I've seen have had a full calendar of new prospect meetings for at least one month into the future, whatever the time of year. It was tough to do, and required discipline and advanced organisational skills to manage it all year round. But it gave them greater performance certainty, and when executed well guaranteed they rarely had to scramble to meet their sales targets.

The next time someone doesn't want to buy from you or defers their decision, listen and learn from them and then move on quickly. Call the next prospect and repeat the process. At the same time, spend time increasing the depth of your sales pipeline and refining your offer. This will ensure you never run out of prospects. Eventually you too will create momentum in your business.

The dual process of 'calling' and 'deepening' are the fundamentals tenets of 'next'—an approach that works no matter what business you are in.

Managing Time

Time is one of those assets you'll never have enough of. There's always too much to do, and not enough time to do it.

But you can make better use of your time. You just need to eliminate the distractions, and use it for the things that will help you achieve your goals.

The Difference Between Important and Urgent

A close colleague of mine once told me he never seemed to have enough time to get everything done. He was always pulling late nights to catch up, and never seemed to get ahead of his work.

Eventually he realised what the problem was—he couldn't differentiate between those activities that were actually important, and those that just seemed to be urgent. Once he realised this and made the changes necessary, his productivity increased dramatically.

US President Dwight Eisenhower once said, "What is important is seldom urgent and what is urgent is seldom important". He went one step further by developing the Eisenhower Matrix to differentiate important activities from the urgent ones.

He defined important activities as having an outcome that leads to achieving your objectives. Conversely urgent activities, while demanding immediate attention, are often associated with achieving someone else's goals rather than your own.

To use Eisenhower's matrix effectively you need to ask two questions whenever a task is presented to you:

1. Is this task urgent?
2. Is this task important?

You then assign the activity to one of four quadrants, depending on your answers:

Quadrant 1 (Urgent and Important)

This is the stress quadrant. The task is both urgent *and* important, and so needs to be acted on immediately. A project might be approaching its deadline, or an unexpected crisis has blown up in your face. Whatever the case, it carries the highest priority for action.

Quadrant 2 (Not Urgent, but Important)

This is the value quadrant. The task at hand isn't urgent (yet), but it's important in terms of achieving your objectives. This is where the organisation's vision and plans get worked on, the team gets developed, and relationships get built. It's the quadrant where you should spend most time because it's where the most company value gets created.

Quadrant 3 (Urgent, but Not Important)

This is the deception quadrant. And is where screw-ups, interruptions and distractions occur. The task is urgent, but not important to achieving the set objectives. If you can, ignore them. If you can't, delegate them to someone else to deal with.

Quadrant 4 (Not Urgent and Not Important)

This is the regret quadrant. This is where time is wasted on activities that don't matter—e.g. checking emails too often, undisciplined 'net surfing or long-winded phone calls.

All Quadrant 4 activities should be discontinued.

Modern business is a pressure cooker, which sometimes makes it difficult to differentiate between the urgent activities and the important ones. We often start dealing with seemingly urgent activities because we get a nasty email, or someone yells down the phone at us demanding our instant attention. We should try to resist attending to urgent matters immediately unless they also qualify as important.

Whatever else, it's a good idea to eliminate quadrant 4 activities altogether and maximise quadrant 2 activities.

Finally, reducing unnecessary urgency in your organisation is a good thing, no matter what else you do.

My Time Management Secrets

Most days I'm at my desk by 8.30am, and I don't get up from it until around noon. My goal is to do a full day's work before lunch, so I set myself a big task to do in this time—something that really matters to my business interests. I never multi-task either. And I don't tolerate any distractions.

Time is precious, so I try to use it well. I can do whatever I want for the rest of the day—business development, future planning, day-to-day stuff or nothing at all if I choose. The pre-lunch discipline gives me that luxury. Even if I have a particularly busy week, I still try to stick to this routine so I'm always moving forward.

I try to check my emails only once or twice a day, and never the first thing in the morning. (I'll admit I'm not perfect at this.) If there's anything urgent I tell people to call me. My mobile phone is always on, but I don't get a lot of *urgent* calls.

I don't like fuss, clutter or waste. Consistent high-quality work is important to me, and I strive for maximum, quality output for minimum input. I also don't let *perfect* get in the way of *better*.

Staying fit, active and healthy with good sleep patterns is also an important ingredient in staying productive, in my experience.

One of the biggest *distractors* can be your mobile phone. And I'm vigilant about it not interrupting my morning schedule. The last thing I need to hear is it beeping away in the background signalling that I've received another email.

People who are 'addicted' to emails operate differently to this. They've convinced themselves it's important to read and respond to email immediately, even if it's unimportant or could wait. My advice is to either defer it or ignore it. By answering it immediately you're prioritising it ahead of everything else you're doing.

I've never understood why it's so important to read or respond to every email immediately. I'd rather get a 'considered' response than a quick one any day.

I also use both a **To Do List** and a **Not To Do List**. Let me explain the difference.

The **To Do List** is about managing priorities, not activities. It's only current for one day, and lists the things you plan to get done today. Any more than 3-4 items is typically too many. All items should be important, and they should all get completed today. Any activity not on the current list should be scheduled for a future To Do List.

Unplanned interruptions are one of the main impediments to completing your daily To Do list. We all have them, and they need to be managed. The trick is to only participate in activities that have a higher priority than those on your To Do List. If they don't, delegate them or defer them. Then focus on the first item on your list. Keep going until it's completed, then move to the next one. If you have priorities of equal rank, divide your time between them.

At the end of each day review your progress against your list. Then prepare a fresh list for tomorrow and start again. At the end of the week, review your overall progress. If you're falling behind, push harder.

The **Not To Do List** is a way to create more time in your day. It should comprise a growing list of activities that free up time so you can work on your To Do List. Here are some common Not to Do List items:

- Making a coffee or having a long chat with your colleagues when you arrive at work.
- Checking email constantly, including first thing in the morning.
- Agreeing to meetings without a clear agenda or timeframe in mind.
- Prolonging the social aspects of business. If someone calls you, ask "What's up?" rather than "How are things with you?" Get to the point quickly.
- Answering the phone if you don't recognise the number. Let it go to voicemail. Decide later whether or not you'll call them back.
- Spending time with time-wasters who can't help you achieve your priorities. (Low-end customers and overly needy staff are prime examples.)
- Handling documents or emails multiple times. Deal with it once and move on.

The only way to stay focused on the critical items on your To Do List is to remove the constant interruptions and distractions in your day. That's why the Not To Do List is so important. The two lists work hand-in-hand to give you the time and focus you need to get the important things done.

You'll be amazed at the difference it can make to your life. You may even discover 3½ hours of uninterrupted time each day to work on those things that really matter.

Just like I did.

Deadlines Are Serious Business

Deadlines need to be taken seriously. They're a promise to deliver, and promises matter. So I don't consider deadlines are just aspirational dates ("I'll do my best to get it done", "I'll see what I can do", etc.) That's not a deadline *or* a promise to deliver.

A guy who worked with me in the '90s (and went on to become a successful senior executive) delights in telling how he got thrown out of my office more times than he can remember for missing deadlines. Eventually he realised my view of deadlines was quite different to most people's. He learned the deadline was when the work was finally completed, *not* when it was 'handed in'. Once he realised this he adjusted his timeframes to make sure he was sitting in front of me with his work 3-4 days *before* the final deadline. He then had time to make any changes before the work was finalised. From that point on he hit his deadlines every time, and was never thrown out of my office again.

I'm genuinely surprised by the number of business people who don't take deadlines seriously. They'll initially agree to it, but then get distracted by other things and either deliver it late or forget about it completely. In their mind they'll justify that most timeframes can be extended, and that it's not a big deal if it's a bit late.

That might be fine if the business operated in a vacuum around a single person, but it doesn't. Any time overruns will create problems and surprises elsewhere in the organisation. The key is to set tough but realistic deadlines, and then aim to complete the work 3-4 days ahead of schedule. This gives everyone time to assess and review the work before it's finalised, which will always lead to better outcomes.

When All Else Fails, Be Dogged

In 2011 I was involved in buying Calendar Club out of voluntary administration following the collapse of Red Group Retail, its owner at the time. It was six weeks of tough, unrelenting work and eventually we only had to sort out one minor matter to complete the deal—getting a routine, written consent from a small counter-party.

Three weeks before we'd received a verbal consent, so getting the written document didn't seem too difficult. But despite daily follow-ups we still hadn't received it.

Out of time, and with the transaction settlement scheduled the next day, I rang the company and was told the document would be ready to be picked up at 1pm. When I arrived it wasn't ready, and I was asked to come back in an hour. I told them it wasn't a problem, and that I'd just wait outside in the street.

To keep their attention I didn't sit down, and instead positioned myself 20 metres away from their front door—close enough to be seen, but far enough away not to be a nuisance.

At 2pm I went back to obtain the document. Still not ready. No problem. I went back to my post. At 3.30pm I went back again and was met by the principal of the company. He apologised for the delay, and asked whether it could be done next week. (Remember, we'd already waited three weeks.)

My response was along the lines of "Take your time. I know these matters are difficult. I'm happy to wait. It's not a problem for me. Do what you need to do. I'll just wait outside until you're done." I went back outside, and three more hours passed with me standing guard. At 6.30pm he re-emerged, tie undone and with a light sheen of sweat on his brow, and said he'd have the document ready by 7pm.

Finally, at 8.30pm, he came out one final time—worn-out and agitated, but with the document in hand. I thanked him profusely and headed home.

It was a miserable, cold day and I'd stood outside for nearly eight hours. But it was a small price to pay for getting a document signed that meant we could now save a great business and protect the livelihoods of numerous loyal and long-standing staff members.

I learnt the trait of doggedness from an old boss in the oil industry. Many times we'd be working on a deal, and two days out from settlement the number of items we still needed to resolve would fill a shopping list. Despite this, my boss rarely agreed to delay the settlement. He encouraged me to use the time pressure to resolve 'hold-out' issues and other minor matters. I still remember how unreasonable I thought he was. But it worked, and we closed more than 80% of our deals on time.

His attitude was simple:

- Set a deadline.
- Don't change it
- Make it clear it has to happen
- Be dogged
- Get it done

Looking back, I realise it would have been easier to extend the deadlines, and I certainly would have liked to. But, most of the time there was no need, as long as were determined and resolute. On the other hand I've seen deals drag on for months due to a lack of focus and discipline, costing everyone money and eroding the opportunity as more time passes.

Standing outside for eight hours in the cold and wet might seem like an extreme way to get a document signed. And it is. But in the end it was necessary to get the deal done on time. And that's what counted.

All it took was a healthy dose of doggedness.

The Time Management Challenge

"Hello. Since coming into the business six months ago as CEO, I've observed the organisation in action and been impressed by what I've seen. But there's one matter, a behavioural one, that I want to tune up to ensure our success continues. Going forward, I intend to manage 'time' as a finite resource in this organisation, just as I would any of our more obvious resources.

"Cutting to the chase, I know many of you work 60 hours or more a week, and have been for years. I'm not convinced it's a good long-term habit, so we're going to change that.

"I want you fresh, motivated and ready to go every single day, not worn out by working yourself into the ground. I want to unlock the full discretionary efforts of the entire team for eight to ten hours a day, and then send you home to enjoy the rest of your life. Some might call this aspirational, and maybe it is, but I'm committed to making it our new reality.

"To do that we need to be laser-focused, and work only on things that matter to our future. Everything else will be jettisoned. This doesn't mean our goals suddenly got easier. They haven't. In fact, our two goals are the same they've always been:

- Achieve our financial objectives
- Ensure our business culture, which is already excellent, improves rather than diminishes.

"To show how serious I am, here's how we'll be operating a week from now:

- The office doors will open at 8am and close at 6pm Monday to Friday.
- No emails will be sent after 7pm.
- You'll only need to be available for around 45 hours a week, not 24/7.
- You'll need to take all of your holidays every year.

"I won't be increasing the organisation's size or structure to achieve our goals. And I'll challenge every method, process, behaviour or habit that gets in the way of us achieving them. I don't expect to get there overnight, but if it takes longer than six to eight months I'll be disappointed.

"I appreciate some of these changes may be painful as we learn how to operate differently. But I won't accept anything less than 100% success. Are my expectations clear?

"Okay. Now, tell me what *you* need to change and what the organisation needs to change to get this done."

Did this actually happen? Maybe, maybe not. I'm not telling, not that it matters anyway. But it's an interesting challenge, and arguably one many organisations could benefit from.

Especially if they want to treat time as a valuable, finite organisational resource.

Crisis Management

No matter how much you plan for emergencies, there's a good chance you'll have to face an unexpected crisis in your business. It won't ever be a pleasant experience but the odds are that it will eventually happen to you, maybe more than once. The speed that you operate and the quality of the decisions you take may be the only protection you have. What do you do next?

Dealing With Chaos And Confusion

Every year my wife and I sit down and think about what we'd like to achieve in the next 12 months. We talk about goals for our family, our personal aspirations and our business interests. We also look back at what we achieved in the previous year. It's an exercise that's always good, mostly fun and occasionally confronting.

A few years ago we had a stellar year on every front, and our plan for the next 12 months was for more of the same. We were excited, hopeful and probably a little bit complacent.

But almost immediately we learnt how quickly things can change.

The unexpected death of a close friend of mine, and the rapid decline of a business in front of our eyes, turned what we'd hoped would be the best year of our lives into one that suddenly looked a lot less promising. A period of prosperity had transformed into one of chaos. Thankfully the business turned around, but I still recall how desperate those times were.

What I learned is you can't control as much as you want to, no matter how hard you try. The world is a complex place, and random events will occur that could delight you or devastate you. What's important is being able to operate effectively in the midst of the chaos and confusion. You can't fall to pieces in the bad times, and you can't pat yourself on the back for too long in the good times. Both are temporary situations, and you'll encounter both as you move through life.

To operate effectively in chaos you must have a couple of important conditions in place.

The first condition is **stability.** Whether it's your personal life or your business life, your underlying internal environment must be stable. In business, this means the internal behaviour of an organisation and its people must be predictable (i.e. predictability about how risks and opportunities are assessed, and how work is prioritised and completed). Even in the darkest times predictable internal behaviour provides a safe haven for a business to rapidly deploy resources to start fixing whatever needs to be fixed.

The second condition is that within this environment of stability people need to be given **freedom** and **autonomy** to operate and more importantly to make decisions knowing they'll sometimes make mistakes.

Expecting people to show initiative won't happen, unless they're given not only freedom to operate but also the support base to encourage them to find the very best solution every time without fear of recrimination.

One thing to avoid is telling people their "balls are on the line so you better not screw up". It *will* produce predictable behaviour, but it will be either risk-averse or too risky—both of which are less than optimal. It's hard enough to operate in chaos without worrying that no-one has your back and your job is on the line. It's better to join hands and fight the battles together.

When unexpected events occur it's important to move quickly to understand what happened and why, and then quickly assess what your options are. Getting used to operating in a chaotic, uncertain environment will become increasingly important in the future, and speed of action will be your greatest defence.

Managing A Crisis

A few years ago I was faced with two business crises. I didn't cause either of them, but I was nevertheless involved and found myself in a lead role trying to save both businesses. Both were messy and desperate situations that could have ended badly if we adopted the wrong approach or moved too slowly.

When confronted with these problems it was hard to know what to do first. The scale of the issues we faced seemed overwhelming, and the timeframe far too short to get everything done that was needed. We had our backs to the wall, and the clock was ticking fast.

We needed to create some clarity, and the only way to do that was to establish a set of business rules that would guide all the decisions we'd need to make. Without rules we felt our progress would be slowed, which in view of the extreme circumstances was something we simply couldn't tolerate.

To that end we deliberated and came up with ten business rules that not only worked for us but subsequently set both businesses up for solid futures.

Here are the rules we used:

- Understand your ultimate objective. That is, what needs to be achieved and by when.
- Focus only on what can be controlled.
- If it doesn't make money, ditch it.
- Challenge anything that makes no commercial sense.
- Hold the team to high performance standards.
- Insist on insights, not just information.
- Don't apologise for any tough but necessary decisions taken.

- Move quickly.
- Don't screw up. Get it right the first time.
- Be prepared to work 24/7 until the crisis subsides.

We knew we had to move quickly—far quicker than we'd normally be comfortable with. But we had no choice. Both situations were desperate, and would deteriorate further unless we took decisive action.

We also made the conscious decision in advance that no matter how much pressure was applied to us we would not fold. No matter what happened. Or how hard it got.

Fortunately we succeeded on both counts because of two things—the quality of our decisions and the speed in which we acted.

The rules were critical in our success. Hopefully they'll help you too when that inevitable crisis moment comes knocking at your door.

Final lesson

Eighty Four Important Things I've Learned In Business.

Well, we're just about at the end of the book. It's been quite a journey for me, and I hope the lessons I've provided can help you with yours.

Thanks for reading, especially if you read the entire book. I really appreciate it, and hope you enjoyed it.

To finish off, I'd like to share 84 important things I've learned in business. Some people have said they want to laminate it and put it on their wall, but I don't expect you to go that far. Just use it in whatever way works best for you.

1. There is no substitute for hard work. *Ever*. Luck always seems to follow the hardest workers.
2. Keep asking yourself – what's my job? If the answer isn't – to satisfy my customers – then repeat the question.
3. What people say about you (whether it's good or bad) is none of your business.
4. Most obstacles can be overcome. Some via a frontal assault, some with stealth and some with patience. The trick is to find the weak point and bash away until it topples over.
5. Be positive. It's rarely as bad as you think.
6. Being cool is (way) overrated. The hipsters, 'movers and shakers', and the 'it' crowd take

themselves far too seriously. Same applies for anyone trying to 'keeping up with the Joneses'. It all seems like bloody hard (pointless) work.

7. Listen to the 'experts', but trust your gut and make your own decisions.
8. The most important thing is how good your product is. Everything else ranks behind that.
9. Trust is not an 'easy commodity. It takes a long time to earn it and a momentary lapse to lose it.
10. Business is a long game, so be fair and ethical with all your business dealings.
11. Customers are 'king' and need to be treated as a precious resource.
12. Meeting deadlines is as important as anything else in business.
13. Business is mostly common sense. The same can't be said of human beings.
14. Network 24/7. You can never know enough people.
15. Never burn bridges. The business community is too small and inter-connected.
16. Don't believe crap like "my word is my bond". Get it in writing.
17. Never work for free. It won't be valued and it won't feed your family.
18. Make sure bad news travels fast. Then fix the problem quickly.
19. Be the best at one thing, not average at many.
20. Scale only occurs when a business is built on rock-solid foundations.
21. Nobody owes you anything. So don't sulk. Instead, figure out how to get what you want.
22. The world is uncertain, so decisions will always need to be made with less than complete information.

23. Slow down. Get it right the first time. Then move on to the next important thing.
24. Sacred cows are bad for business. So is the status quo.
25. Change is inevitable, so get used to it.
26. Theory is nice. But hard experience is better.
27. Meetings should be short and achieve something worthwhile.
28. Don't confuse what's urgent with what's important.
29. If you don't know what to do, ask for help.
30. "Just be better than you were yesterday" is a great organisational strategy.
31. The worst-case scenario rarely happens. But you should prepare for it anyway.
32. Invest sensibly based on a good understanding of the risk, but never punt.
33. Don't outsource anything valuable or that you care about.
34. Hustle. If you're not talking to your customers regularly there's a good chance someone else is.
35. Hire well and slowly but fire fast.
36. Be nice.
37. Don't employ yes-men, narcissists, lazy types or fence sitters. Employ people who will argue with you and challenge you to be better and do better.
38. Achieving success is hard. Bloody hard. But it's worth it.
39. Talk is cheap. Make it crystal clear what you will *and* won't do. Then do it.
40. It's not about being right. It's about making progress.
41. Sweat the small stuff (before it becomes the big stuff).
42. Don't lie. *Ever.*

43. Only do things you'd be proud to tell your family about.
44. Ideas are cheap. Execution is everything.
45. Pay everyone on time, every time.
46. Make no apologies for expecting your debtors to pay on time.
47. Don't Blame. Learn instead and move on quickly. You can't change mistakes. Do better next time.
48. Create a Hero culture. Publicly praise and reward the heroes in your business. They'll love it and the others will want to be it.
49. Steal Business. From your competitors. Pick off the ones that take their customers for granted.
50. Getting press coverage is easy. But most of it isn't worth the effort.
51. Just be yourself. If you're different at work than at a BBQ you're faking it.
52. Mistakes are okay. Just don't make the same ones twice.
53. Stay young, even when the years start mounting up.
54. Laugh. Smile. Tell funny jokes and stories. Be the happiest person at work.
55. Ask the dumb questions to avoid making the dumb mistakes.
56. Costs matter. Every last cent. Only spend money on what makes you more money.
57. Measure Everything. If you don't measure it you can't control it.
58. Every time you cancel a meeting or don't deliver what you promise adds to your reputation as a 'flake'. That's bad.
59. Innovate even when you don't need to.
60. Conflict is inevitable. But it must lead to reconciliation.

61. Set a great personal example and never be afraid to get your hands dirty.
62. Money doesn't buy influence, or friends, that last. If you need to 'pay to play' then you'll find yourself easily replaceable by the next dude with a bigger wallet. And there are always plenty of those. Instead, be someone special with unique skills that people really want.
63. If you think you're important or have 'made it', you're wrong.
64. People lie on their CVs.
65. Do it now. Before nightfall. Stop stuffing around.
66. Communicate everything important DAILY to EVERYONE, not just the inner circle.
67. Not everything is worth learning.
68. When a taxi driver gives you stock tips, sell everything FAST. The bubble is about to burst.
69. The media isn't your friend – they're agnostic - they'll write about you equally if you've won the lottery or are going to jail. Then they'll move on to the next story.
70. Don't be an out of date business doing out of date things.
71. People only change when *they* want to.
72. The ability to influence others is a key requirement to be successful.
73. It doesn't have to be perfect. It just has to be really good.
74. Pick up the phone if you want to talk to the Prime Minister or Warren Buffett. They might answer.
75. Get face to face with your customers and suppliers. Regularly. Consider it mandatory education.
76. Bring your A-Game. To every meeting, phone call and other interaction. The "big" deal is coming. Be ready.

77. Your supply chain is the backbone of your business and should be a huge generator of profit.
78. Don't brag about your accomplishments or (importantly) exaggerate them. Instead spend your time doing more and achieving more.
79. Always work all the angles and think strategically.
80. Be able to say "You can count on me" and mean it because it is true.
81. Do the right thing because it's the right thing to do.
82. Add more value than you're using up. (In other words, give more than you take).
83. Tomorrow is a new day. Make it your best one ever.

And finally, the last one. And it's really important:

84. You'll never be (quite) ready…

- To grab that opportunity.
- To start that business.
- To quit that job.
- To hire (or fire) that person.
- To pivot and change direction.
- To do that first keynote.
- To write that book.
- To get married.
- To have children.
- To go on that adventure.
- To face that painful truth.
- To confront that bully.
- To quit smoking, booze or drugs.
- To deal with that personal foible.

- To get off the couch.

Or to make any other tough decision you *know* you should make.

So what?

Life is a messy and chaotic collision of circumstances and opportunities – good and bad. And the pieces will never line up perfectly before you decide to make that leap of faith that will propel you forward.

You'll never be ready if you keep waiting for the perfect time to come.

Get ready enough.

Then do it.

That makes you ready.

It's time to get started…

Bibliography

Built to Last: Successful Habits of Visionary Companies by Jim Collins and Jerry Porras (1994).

The Likeability Factor: How to Boost Your L Factor & Achieve your Life's Dreams by Tim Sanders (2006)

The Power of Ethical Management by Ken Blanchard and Norman Vincent Peale (1988)

The Art of War by Sun Tzu (~500 BC)